Writing to Win

Writing to Win

Mel Lewis

McGraw-Hill Book Company

London · New York · St Louis · San Francisco · Auckland
Bogotá · Guatemala · Hamburg · Lisbon · Madrid · Mexico
Montreal · New Delhi · Panama · Paris · San Juan
São Paulo · Singapore · Sydney · Tokyo · Toronto

Published by
McGRAW-HILL Book Company (UK) Limited
MAIDENHEAD · BERKSHIRE · ENGLAND

British Library Cataloguing in Publication Data
Lewis, Mel
  Writing to win.
  1. English language—Business English
  2. English language—Writing
  I. Title
  808'.066651021   PE1115

  ISBN 0-07-084942-0 SC
  ISBN 0-07-707095-X HC

Library of Congress Cataloguing in Publication Data
Lewis, Mel.
  Writing to win.
  Bibliography: p.
  Includes index.
  1. English language—Business English.   2. Commercial
correspondence.   I. Title.
PE1115.L49   1987   808'.066651   87-22586
ISBN 0-07-084942-0 SC
ISBN 0-07-707095-X HC

2345   JWA   898

Typeset by Eta Services (Typesetters) Ltd, Beccles, Suffolk
and printed and bound in Great Britain by
J. W. Arrowsmith Limited, Bristol

To my much-loved family, Eddy
and our son Jack.
You took it on the jaw with this
one.

Contents

Preface

This book won't turn you into a good writer in the classroom sense of developing a fine prose style ... punctuating properly ... observing the 'rules' of grammar ... and so on. In fact you may need to abandon a few school rules and become something of a writing renegade, on your road to more professional and profitable business writing. What *Writing to Win* will show you, step by revealing step, is how to become a more *effective* writer as far as your own business is concerned.

You'll learn ... how to write a business letter that doesn't waste the reader's—or your own—valuable time ... how to pen publicity and sales copy that builds confidence and cements business relationships ... how to produce illustrated material—from a letterhead to an instant print leaflet to a full colour magazine-style catalogue—that projects an image of your business that is the best possible one, given your type of trade, the competition, your objectives, and also takes prudential account of your resources for funding printed promotional initiatives.

In addition, I explain how a professional tackles the writing of proposals and reports, and give advice on how to write a better advertisement—and show you how to monitor the advertising copy that agencies produce on your behalf.

Advertising that entertains, gets talked about and wins awards may ensure more business for the agency that produces it—but brings little in the way of trade to the door of the customer who commissions and pays for it. As you must have noticed, people take parting with their cash very seriously indeed, so they appreciate ads that don't fool about. A big businessman once remarked that half of the money he spent on advertising was money down the drain; but he could never work out which half. Reading this book you will discover how to write—or elicit and personally edit—advertising, both halves of which are working hard, and cost-effectively, on your behalf.

Although this book is in no way a course book, it will teach you things of considerable commercial value to you. Such as how to promote your own business in the national and local Press. Journalists and editors are busy people, but they are generally not *business* people. They have pages to fill, not coffers. Therefore you need to talk to them in a particular way and, most of all, you must give them what they want in the form they want it, when they want it.

I refer, of course, to writing Press releases, and an entire and substantial chapter is devoted to this little understood craft. Good Press publicity is worth wooing on a good many counts, but most of all because it is *free*!

Mel Lewis
London

Acknowledgements

No writer ever received more help, inspiration and sheer impetus to become truly *professional* than I did from Lou de Swart, my friend and mentor for 16 years. 'You're a good man with a word', Lou once told me. Lou was better, with more words.

No one helped more with the shaping of this particular book than Peter George, Director of Operations of The Porchester Group and one of the finest editors I ever met.

I would also like to thank the following who have kindly given permission to reproduce examples of their publicity work:

Dragons of Walton Street Ltd, *The London Evening Standard*, Aminatta Forna, Gino Giorgi, Halifax Building Society, *The Independent*, Duncan J. MacLean, Miller & Kendall, Music Sales Ltd, Pitt & Scott Ltd, PNA, The Porchester Group, Smith Bundy & Partners Ltd, Southwark Computer Services.

Mel Lewis

1. *Professional pointers*

It's clear from a lot of writing, especially advertising, even by highly-paid professionals, that many writers have never read a book on the subject. There are a great many good books on writing, most of them American, and these are listed in the back of the book. Or these people have read the right books but have forgotten the things they were told.

The answer is to study works by masters of the craft you wish to perfect—and then re-read them. Not only will you freshen your memory, but you'll also, often, discover something you didn't see first time around.

Books are, of course, only part of the learning process, albeit a vital part. I see the essential pattern like this: *study ... practise ... put into practice.* The funny thing is, many people do implement the three parts of this improvement plan but they still don't improve. Or they get better, but never really quite make it to the top.

Let me give you an example. Many people (*especially* men, for some reason) are keen photographers. They read up on the subject, they devour photography magazines, they understand the equipment, keep up to date with technical developments, they even follow the advice that is given and shoot lots of rolls of film. They may even end up taking some good photographs.

What they discover, though, is that they can't *guarantee* results. Sometimes they're hot shots, sometimes they lose a few foreheads.

The professional photographer has a similar problem producing top-notch work every time—leastways, it's not really a problem. Because the one thing the pro is sure of is being *GOOD ENOUGH*. Paid practitioners learn their craft in the real world where 'not good enough' either goes unpaid, or doesn't get asked twice.

You may be in a position where you are not perpetually on the rack of being 'only as good as your last assignment'. Lucky you! But being in business, your writing mettle *can* be tested in a commercial context. Therefore you *do* have the opportunity to get seriously good at business writing.

But don't take just my word for this, or anything. Read the work of other professionals. Study what other writers say on the *same* subject. Not only will what they say start to sink in, but you'll also start to *believe* what they say. On that note, a little story.

One of my client companies has working for it a Grade A salesman: we'll call him Stuart. Stuart and I were having a discussion about mortgages. Which sort was best, I wanted to know; which could he recommend. Stuart mentioned another person known to us, a founder director of that same company. Stuart had been anxious to know the answer to the same question and had asked the millionaire director which mortage was best in her opinion, one he knew he must value highly, since she had substantial property interests in the West End of London and a luxurious holiday home abroad.

Back came the answer: 'I don't know my dear. I've never had one.'

From that point on, Stuart didn't need to take a degree in mortgages. In fact, he didn't need to ask anyone another thing about them. He admired and respected this successful woman, and if something was financially good enough for her, as he was aiming to be a millionaire himself, it was good enough for him, too. Today, Stuart owns *three* properties with *no* mortgages.

People are always saying, 'You'll learn by your mistakes'—and so you will. But you'll progress a lot faster, and surer, if you let other people make mistakes for you.

Getting better—a word of warning

Learning new techniques is an exciting experience. Most intelligent people thrill to the prospect of getting more skilful, more efficient—in a word, more *professional*—at the various things they do. And if those new techniques relate to their work, and getting better results in doing more business and earning more money, then that is a bonus and a double benefit.

For a short while, however, while a new technique is assimilated, the person might actually get worse, not better, at something they have been doing well enough for years. A mundane example will help.

A lot of car drivers cross their hands on the steering wheel when turning the corners. They weren't taught to do that, and they certainly wouldn't have passed their test doing it. That sloppy habit, is, of course, *dangerous*: in an emergency one would not be fully in control; those split seconds could cost a life; and so on.

However, people slip into bad habits, when bad habits are good enough most of the time. Now if drivers, for whatever reason, decide to retrain to steer properly—with hands fixed at the '10 to two' position, feeding the wheel round when turning corners—then for a short while, at least, they will go through a period when they will be *more* dangerous as a driver, while they master the new (forgotten) technique. Our drivers may even start to get anxious about the whole business of driving.

Let me now try to relate this example to business writing. My understanding is that business people do not, as a breed, agonize about their writing. They just get on with it. It may not be as good as it could be ... It may not even be as good as it needs to be (in which case, money and time are wasted, no new business comes in, and so on) ... but the business executive does *not* normally suffer from writer's block.

Now I suspect that as you assimilate and, hopefully, practise, the various techniques, and experiment with the ideas this book contains, you will find writing a more onerous activity—at least in the short term.

You'll be thinking more about what you set down, how it looks, and so on; and also, you will *worry* about the end result, so you may slow up, or even come to a halt.

Professional writers regularly agonize about their work; they want to produce the best piece of writing possible for the job in hand. But at a pinch, they also know when to cut the cackle, swallow their anxieties (perhaps with a slug of whisky, to help) and *get on with it*.

The amateur writer, like the professional, sometimes comes up with something brilliant. The difference between the two is that the pro will always pull out of the hat something that is *good enough*. That, then, is the goal to aim for.

Learn how to let your thoughts run riot

Whether you are agonizing over a headline ... the entire contents of a sales letter ... the selling points of a brochure ... or even an intriguing way of writing the opening sentence of a memo ... it pays to research your options. Often, the best source of research material is already in your possession—between your ears. It just needs to be coaxed a little.

Letting your mind wander sounds fun, and easy. But it may not be, not all the time. Some people get 'thought-tied' the way others get tongue-tied. We are taught to be such proper little creatures of habit and order and good taste, which can be a handicap where this kind of free-ranging mental activity is concerned.

I find it helps to get in the mood. That can mean anything from lying on a bed, propped against a wedge of pillows, with a clipboard of paper and my favourite writing instrument. Or it can call for a walk with notebook in hand—there's something very inspiring and relaxing about walking where you don't have to keep worrying about avoiding pedestrians or traffic. So a large park or the countryside is ideal.

Sometimes a drink or two helps spin the cogs. I used to drink with Tim Aspinall, the playwright and scriptwriter, at a favourite Young's pub on the River Lea in Hackney. It was the birthplace of at least one episode of *Coronation Street*, as a matter of interest! Tim knew his limits, however, anything over two pints and that was the end of work for the afternoon. Given the temptation, his willpower was remarkable.

It may help to work with other people who have shown the right kind of temperament and verbal flair. Bouncing around ideas at a 'creative session' can produce better, quicker results than one person nibbling a pencil alone could manage. In fact, this type of activity is organized on a professional basis by two firms, Novamark and Interbrand. They recruit promising silver-tongued individuals to help dream up the catchy brand names on washing powder, face cream, and so on, at specially convened brain-storming sessions.

Vanessa Leigh, an account executive in the City section of Press release distribution company PNA, is one such wordsmith. (She is also the author of a book entitled *The Pocket Guide to Men*, which sold over 13 000 copies in three months, as I write!) And the cartoonist (and illustrator of that book) Brian West, is also in demand at these sessions.

The fee is nominal, I gather, but the booze runs free. Not only does this *ad hoc* committee have a lot of fun, but they also produce results, which are then run through a computer, tested in market research surveys, and so on, before being adopted for branded goods. Here are just three of their successes: Barbican, the alcohol-free lager; the Mini Metro car and Quatro the soft drink. If brain-storming is right for professionals working for multi-nationals might it not work for you and your business?

Cultivate a 'listening post'

A 'listening post' is someone who reads your writing (or listens to you speaking your lines), who says little, knows when something is right and when it's not, who means well, but is not afraid to tell you when what you've penned is a crock of shoe polish.

Where do you find such paragons? Hard to say—try asking your business friends if they have an unfinished novel in the bottom drawer somewhere. What you want is someone who appreciates language, understands business objectives, and knows when (if not how) the two mesh.

Why do you need one? Because in the early stages of learning how to be a better business writer at least, you are unlikely to be able to 'distance' yourself from your prose; the necessary detachment comes with experiences, study, practice, and most of all, success. Nothing sucks eggs like a grandmother, and nothing speeds progress quite like success.

2. Getting to grips with the nuts and bolts of writing

This morning (as I write), I went to a 'Parent Teacher Children Association' session at my five-year-old son's school. The meeting was mainly about the children's 'Readers', a series of books designed to set them on the road to reading. One book had a 50-word story on the left-hand page for the parent to read to its child, and on the right-hand page a very brief resumé for the child to have a stab at, having heard the parent explain the story.

The teacher chairing the meeting read us the little story in one of the books. It was all about a cat that kept falling in its saucer of milk. The child's version, which showed a picture of the milk-splattered kitten read, simply, 'SILVER IN ITS SAUCER'.

The teacher immediately apologized for this 'ungrammatical' sentence: 'It should be, "SILVER IS IN ITS SAUCER".'

Should it? Why? Why is it acceptable for me to write 'Why?' as a sentence. Where is the verb here? My one-word sentence is, of course, eliptical; it's short for 'why is it acceptable?'

'Ah ... but that's only speech', I hear. No it isn't, that's writing: you just read it, you didn't hear it. Perhaps I should not have written it at all. That is a different story. In that case, you would also have to censure *The Times* ... *Reader's Digest* ... American Express ... Shakespeare; important publications, respected companies and famous writers, all, *all* take liberties with language. They are happy to break the rules of grammar because the people who read their prose are themselves rule breakers. In fact, going by the rule book can lead to unfamiliar-sounding, stilted writing. What was accepted form in Edwardian times is considered stiff today. If you want people to warm to your writing, to *respond* to it, then you should try to give it a familiar feel. That doesn't mean using sloppy constructions, jargon, slang or ugly contractions, such as 'ain't'. It does mean being flexible and not afraid of trying something for effect.

After all, the reason the big name companies mentioned above write their sales letters the way they do is simple: such letters work for them. The truth is, that companies like Time-Life and *Reader's Digest* built their fortunes on subscription-getting letters that are models of controlled modern writing that gives all the illusion of being familiar, friendly language.

Pulling out the stops—and putting them back in again
The best business writing is crisp writing. Never use long words where short ones will do—according to the late, great wordsmith Lou de Swart. Lou wrote:

> *In order to achieve anything at all, you have to 'keep 'em reading'.* That means making what you write *easy* to read. Easy reading may be hard writing. But as a writer in business it's your job to make it as easy on the reader as possible. Remember: you are not trying to write great literature. Your letters are written to *express*—not impress.
>
> American advertising writers—the best of them, that is—have a rule. It goes something like this 'Don't use 10-dollar words, use 5 cent ones. Write it for the Smiths and the Smythes will get the message, too'. Wise words. What goes for advertising, goes for letters. If you've got business letters with mile-long words, put a pencil through those words this minute. And put half-inch words in their place. You'll be surprised how much easier it reads, how much crisper and snappier it sounds.

Remember, the people who want to read your letters and ads are MOVING TARGETS. They read on the train or bus to work ... and again on their way home ... they read over lunch ... between television programmes. People who read like that haven't time to figure out high-flown language. It isn't that they can't read it—lots of them can. They've just got so many other things to do in this busy day and age.

If you want them to stop knitting, stop talking to their fellow passengers, stop trying to solve crosswords—and listen to you—BE UNDERSTANDING. Write so that they don't need a dictionary every other word.

People sometimes write long sentences, using long words, when they have a complicated idea to put across. What happens is that the sentence is written 'at the run'. As if the writer was afraid of pausing for fear of losing the thread of the argument. But while there may be relief for the writer, having got the thoughts on paper, there is nothing but grief for the reader, who then has to unravel the badly-expressed 'difficult' concept.

Perhaps you have heard it said, that if you can't explain something you don't really know it. If putting something into words makes you anxious, go over the facts. Make sure you really know what you are talking about—on paper, if necessary—then try writing the sentence again.

Never let your reader long for the end of a sentence. Break down a very long sentence into several short ones. Short sentences are easier to read than long sentences. But a string of short sentences act on the brain like rat-tat-tapping on a window—they irritate. So vary the length of sentences, alternating short ones—eight to five words, or less—with longer ones.

The best business writing uses a lot of punctuation. Not for its own sake. But because, if you follow my advice, you will be using shorter sentences ... clearer layouts, with specific points set out by being indented. With dashes or asterisks to signal the start of each fresh message or idea.

Every shred of experience tells us that people don't like hard work. They like to take things in in easy instalments. That applies to food—chocolate buttons, fish fingers, TV programmes sprinkled with commercial *breaks*. It applies also to reading, and therefore to writing.

That is not to say you should use masses of punctuation for its own sake. There has been a drive to clear unnecessary punctuation out of business correspondence. So instead of writing:

> Mr. Mel Lewis,
> 2, Dagmar Passage,
> London, N1 2DN.

We now write:

> Mel Lewis
> 2 Dagmar Passage
> London N1 2DN

We do this for the same reason that we no longer set out the address thus:

> Mel Lewis,
>   2, Dagmar Passage,
>   London, N1 2DN.

Today we write

> Dear Mr Lewis

and sign off:

> Yours sincerely

set to the same extreme left-hand margin as the rest of the letter.

Instead of:

> Dear Mr. Lewis:

or

> Dear Mr Lewis:

with the sign-off set over to the right side of the paper:

> Yours sincerely

This style is preferred largely because *it saves time.*

Staggering lines, showering copy with non-essential commas and full stops *wastes time.* And nowadays, secretarial time is an expensive consideration for any business.

There is another reason, however. If something is obvious, we say, 'there's no need to dot the "i's" and cross the "t's"' (ignoring the fact that it should really be 'is' and 'ts'; after all, the plural of 'legs' is not 'leg's'! More important is what *looks* right. The same with punctuation, in correspondence especially. The so-called 'open punctuation' is preferred today where the meaning is clear enough without labouring the point.

The liberal use of punctuation I advocate is to aid clarity; to sustain or alter rhythm; create mood; ram home a message; or simply to chop up a long list into more easily digestible portions.

I'll say that again. The liberal use of punctuation I advocate is for another reason entirely. It is to aid clarity. To sustain or alter rhythm. Create mood. Ram home a message. Or simply to chop a list into more easily digestible portions.

Which version do you prefer? The one with the semicolons? Or the one using only full points? I believe the second version has a clearer look to it—especially if you leave extra 'white' between the sentences.

But if I had to write several paragraphs with a similar content, I wouldn't be rigid about it. I would write one paragraph using full stops (or points, as some people call them), the other broken up by semicolons. And toss a coin for the next paragraph. So let's take a closer look.

11

Full stops

This isn't a text book. It's a hand book. A guide book. I've put the grammar book, the *rule* book to one side. But I refer constantly to my style book—which happens to be contained entirely in my head.

If my every instinct, honed on over 20 years in journalism, authoring and copywriting tells me that's the way something should be written, then I give myself the benefit of the doubt without going to a 'higher source'. I trust you will do the same, at least for the duration of this brief, heretical seminar.

Full stops, then, end sentences. But forget all you've heard about sentences, about clauses, verbs, subjects, and so on. As far as I am concerned a sentence is whatever you or I care to put in front of a full stop. Or question mark. Or exclamation mark. Okay?

If you've had some sort of education you already know that 'okay?' is an eliptical sentence, short for something like, 'Is the statement made in the previous sentence agreeable to you?' But you also know from everyday life that 'Okay?' is a perfectly acceptable spoken and written form, too, and therefore needs no further justification.

The problem with full stops is not so much when to use them, as when not to ... when to use a colon, or, as we've seen, a semicolon, for preference. Look at the following old-fashioned style of business letter:

> We acknowledge receipt of your letter of 23 September and have to inform you that the policy you are enquiring about was not to hand when you first wrote to us, but you will be pleased to know that we have now ascertained that the ABC Company are issuing it within the next seven days and as soon as it arrives we will despatch it to you.

Phew! Yet you can read sentences like that and worse, day in and day out in business letters.

Now look at it re-written:

Thank you for your letter of 23 September. When your first letter reached us, your policy had not been issued. We have now heard from the ABC Company that we will have it within the next seven days. As soon as it arrives, we will send it to you (by first class post).

A few words have been added so that the last sentence doesn't sound too abrupt. Apart from the first full stop (after 'September') all the others (apart from the closing point) could have been semicolons. Why weren't they?

Because the letter is doing nothing other than transmitting information. If that can be done using crystal clear, discrete, 'snap-off' sentences, then fine.

Semicolons

Semicolons have two main functions. Either they are used for variety's sake, where you have been using too many full stops. Or to set down a long list, usually preceded by a *colon*—although more and more these days, writers separate the various items in a list not with semicolons, but with commas: they have a cleaner look.

The other reason is a stylistic one, where you are trying to sustain rhetoric; where you want to bring your reader almost to a halt, but only to bring down the curtain on one image or idea, in order to pile on the pressure with the next idea, after the semicolon; and so on. Novelists and playwrights use this technique time and again. As a writer in business you will use it rarely.

In fact, there is every reason to treat semicolons with great respect, as well as restraint. In the hands of the expert they become a powerful tool. In the hands of the beginner they are a mighty blunderbuss. As much as full stops signal the close of an idea, so semicolons suggest a *connection* of ideas. For example:

I prefer this colour. Brown suits you.

The colour the writer is referring to could be orange or cyclamen. However

> I prefer this colour; brown suits you.

is another matter entirely. Here the assumption must be that 'colour' and 'brown' are one and the same. The writer is really saying something like, 'I like this colour brown on you'.

How commas can rescue your reader from a quandary
It will always pay you to save your reader work—especially as people in business are also *busy* people. So don't leave your readers scratching their heads. A confused reader is often an impatient one. The typical response of a reader who is both irritated and busy is to skip what is causing the frustration. That may mean turning the page on your report, letter or advertisement, wasting your time, money and effort.

The smallest piece of writing can 'throw' a reader. Take a common comma as in this sentence:

> Our firm manufactures wire wool and sawdust.

Does this mean the firm makes 'wire'? No. To say that you must write:

> Our firm manufactures wire, wool and sawdust.

The comma following 'wire' clears up the confusion with 'wire wool', which the company appears to be making in the first example. You could also put a comma after 'wool', but the modern tendency is to omit the comma before the closing 'and' at the end of a list.

Punctuation tells a reader to slow down or stop. A comma is a 'slow down' signal. If you are ever in doubt where a comma should go, try reading your writing out loud and see where you pause naturally—and also where you are obliged to slow up in order to make your meaning crystal clear.

Whenever I start thinking a loud banging in my head forces me to stop.

The confusion here is aided and abetted by the words 'a loud' which could easily be read as 'aloud'. But the sense is made plain by inserting a comma, thus:

Whenever I start thinking, a loud banging in my head forces me to stop.

Phrases and clauses at the start of sentences, like the previous example, are often the cause of confusion. Likewise when a separate idea is contained in the *middle* of a sentence:

The managing director left to control the new company made a remarkable success of his responsibility.

It's a pound to a penny that the reader will launch into this sentence under the initial impression that the managing director picked up his P45 and walked out the door. Whereas what the MD did do was rise to the occasion, as the inserted punctuation makes obvious:

The managing director, left to control the new company, made a remarkable success of his responsibility.

The phrase 'left to control the new company' is an added ingredient to the main point of the sentence, which stands up quite well on its own:

The managing director made a remarkable success of his responsibility.

Clauses within commas can be critically important to the sense of your sentence.

The evidence suggests that all our market research based on the Rorschach test is flawed.

According to the sentence above, the market research based on questionnaires, lie-detector tests—or what have you, may have been fine, but poor old Rorschach blotted his copybook.

If you want to say that *all* of the research was naff, and incidentally it was a Rorschach programme entirely, you must write:

> The evidence suggests that all our market research, based on the Rorschach test, is flawed.

As I say, I like using a lot of punctuation. It sparks up your copy, makes it move, easier to read, because well-punctuated writing looks more digestible. In fact, when in doubt I prefer to use extra punctuation rather than leave it out.

Traditionally openings such as:

> Firstly, . . .
> Occasionally, . . .
> Finally, . . .

have been followed, as they are in the above examples, with commas. Some writers leave them out arguing that, as the words come so close to the start of the sentence, there is not yet any need to pause for breath—and the sense is obvious enough. Whenever I see such commas left out I want to pencil them in. However, the choice is a stylistic one and yours to make.

Some insertions of commas, however, are not a matter of choice, but a matter of commonsense. How often have you seen the following, or something similar to it?

> Leader of the Opposition, Neil Kinnock, was invited to Buckingham Palace . . .

There are two ways of understanding why these commas are redundant. The first is to see if removing the bit in the middle, 'Neil Kinnock', leaves us with a grammatical expression.

Leader of the Opposition was invited to Buckingham Palace.

It's almost right, and would be perfectly acceptable if it had said '*The* leader of the Opposition . . .'. But all we have is 'Leader'.

Look at it another way. 'Leader of the Opposition' is a descriptive phrase. It tells us a bit more about Neil Kinnock. And it does so rather as if we had said:

Red-haired Neil Kinnock was invited to Buckingham Palace.

You certainly would not want to put:

Red-haired, Neil Kinnock, was invited to Buckingham Palace.

The 'double dot' that keeps the reader on his toes
I feel about colons, somewhat the same way I do about cheese knives. It's nice to have the right tool for the job, but the truth is, another sort of knife will do just as well. The other sort of knife, in punctuation is, of course, the full stop.

The next time you come across a colon, try rewriting the sentence using a full stop to make two sentences. Nine times out of ten the stop will do fine.

But when you abandon rules, as when you establish them, there are exceptions.

Colons are often used to introduce direct quotes (or an example, as here):

The company secretary said: 'I've had enough figure-work for today.'

Often, but not always. You can also use a comma:

The company director said, 'I've had enough figure-work for today.'

Or even run straight into the quotation:

17

> The company director said 'I've had enough figure-work for today.'

The use of quotes is indication enough that the rhythm of the writing has changed.

In a piece of writing where a lot of conversation or a quotation is introduced, from the visual aspect it pays to vary which punctuation you use before quotes.

The colon is also a signal to stop, not quite as abruptly as a full stop, and maybe a bit more than a semicolon. But punctuation is not like musical notation. You can fix a figure on how many crotchets are to be played to the minute in music. But you can't be so precise with grammar.

Besides which, as well as telling you to stop, the colon can also act as a curtain raiser. It says, something is missing from this sentence and here it comes.

> There is only one thing to do: suck it and see.

Curtain raiser is an apt description. The pause the reader gives to a colon is also meant to be a meaningful one, to have *dramatic* effect. So although a full stop would be adequate:

> There is only one thing to do. Suck it and see.

It lacks the 'showmanship' of the colon, which seems to say, this sentence has a punchline and, biff!—here it is!

Occasionally, however, there is little enough difference between using a full stop or a colon, yet still we choose the colon. Why? Take a look at this sentence.

> Our 'winner' prepared an ad that told it all: X brand bottles were 'Thoroughly, hygienically steam cleaned'.

You could substitute a full stop for the colon. But then you'd be left with a sentence beginning with 'X', and that looks uncomfortable. In fact, professional writers go out

18

of their way to avoid starting sentences with bare figures (or letters). Better than writing:

23 directors resigned at that meeting

it would be more stylish to put

Twenty-three directors resigned at that meeting.

Another way to sidestep the ugliness of starting a sentence with figures is to put a word or two in front of the figures

In all, 23 directors resigned at the meeting.

Writing with a dash
Some business writers find something hick about the dash. A dash may be typed as '– –' or even '– – –' in a typescript to avoid confusion with the hyphen. In print, the dash may appear as ' – ' or as '—'. The shorter of these two usually has space either side, the longer butts against the letters. The hyphen is shorter than either and always butts against the letters.

Perhaps the dash recalls all those sales letters trotted out by the sackload by *Reader's Digest*, American Express, *et al*. You know, the ones no one owns up to reading, yet, curiously, enabled such companies, and others like them, to grow to become mega-businesses. . . .

The great thing about the dash is that with practice, you can sustain sentences without losing momentum, something much harder to achieve using commas or colons.

You've seen—or heard about—all those disaster movies (earthquakes, fires, floods, killer fish)—and you must have asked yourself the question: what would I have done? . . . would I—would my family—have survived?

More commonly, the dash has a number of specific uses.

1. To point up an expression repeated for emphasis:

We have never—*never*—achieved such results.

2. To indicate a sudden pause, break or change in thought:

> Those are our normal terms—but, of course, you may prefer to pay cash and collect the discount.

3. In front of a phrase or word which sums up what has already been said:

> The ability to organize oneself—direct others—write effectively—to speak well—to make sound decisions—to get things done—these are the mark of the successful businessman.

4. To set off an explanatory statement:

> The shirkers—those who failed to make six sales calls a day—were soon weeded out.

Dots that keep your audience in suspense

Part of the function of grammar, to a business writer, is, as I say, showmanship. As you have seen, the colon both slows your reader to a temporary halt, and also says 'Hold it . . . here comes the punch line!'

As you have just seen (in my last sentence) dots can also have a theatrical impact. Picture the compere at a circus, or in an old-fashioned music hall, introducing an act, and wanting to generate enthusiasm for the appearance of the next performer.

The compere is trying to whip up excitement among the audience, so the applause will be deafening—even if the entertainer is a complete unknown!—so at least the audience is in the mood to enjoy themselves. And also, of course, the performer gets off on the right foot.

The compere says 'Presenting the greatest . . . the most wonderful . . . bravest . . . most exciting . . . horse-riding duo you have ever seen . . . ladies and gentlemen, I give you

... the Phenomenal Fandagos!' Or something to that effect.

Of course it doesn't have to be so brash. To appreciate just how smooth such presentations can be, just listen to television personalities David Frost or Terry Wogan introducing their guest stars. If you had to transcribe such spiels, sensational or suave, the eulogy would be broken up using dots: '...'.

The dots help build tension, as in this example of a sales letter from The National Research Bureau Inc, of Chicago:

> *You've got money coming* ... from past due accounts. And here is a simple, *proved-effective* way to collect cash ... *at practically no collection cost*!

The firm produces vivid sticky labels to attach to reminder bills to tell slow payers that their time is nigh.

A sales letter that works, very often does so because it successfully mirrors the spoken word. Good salespeople know how to pile it on ... how to fan the flames of desire for the product or service they are selling.

Market Trader Maestro

A couple of years ago I was asked to cover the 'Pitcher of the Year' competition for *Campaign* magazine. Pitchers are ace stand-up sales representatives, usually in an open-air market. They aim to attract a goggle-eyed crowd of punters to buy their wares. To this end, they must grab their interest, sustain it through a riveting demonstration, and then close the sale.

At a (usually) brash level, here is the entire rule book of selling writ small. I was reporting the event, and was also taking photographs of these masterly displays, and in order to be spot-on accurate, I taped the various pitchers in full flood.

One man in particular caught my eye and ear. He was 'Mr Donelly of the Penporium, Purveyor of Quality

Writing Instruments'. His sensational patter—for a range of hi-tech pens—was music to a business writer's ear. In fact, he was so good at his selling job that he sold out before the judging and disappeared, with his profits, before collecting the prize that must have been his.

Writing up this man's successful patter, I was obliged to make use of the entire panoply of punctuation to capture the mood, force and timing of this master of salesmanship.

'This is the best selling pen in the United States. If you drop it, don't worry: our nibs are iridium steel. Iridium is a metal designed as part of the space programme. It's proven so strong and resilient that it's ideal for fountain pens [throws the pen dart-like into a pad of paper, thrusts it through the side of an empty beer can]. Don't try that with a Parker! The only difference between our pen and the Parker is ... ours is unbreakable.

I've been selling these pens for seven months. I'll be quite candid with you, ladies and gentlemen, it's the best pen I've ever had. [He begins to write with a pen]. If you're right-handed, it's ideal; if you're left-handed, it's ideal. It doesn't matter if you're back-handed, cack-handed, or even, like my bank manager, underhanded ....

You can buy this pen in any one of 62 House of Fraser stores. In a fancy box with the company motif on the front, this pen retails at £9.99. When you think about it, for the only pen you're going to need in your life, £10 is not expensive.

But I'm not going to ask you £10. I'm not going to give you a box. Forget about fancy boxes. And forget about fancy prices. I'll give you the fountain pen in a bag. I'll give you the lifetime guarantee, same guarantee you'll get if you pay £10.

But instead of charging you £10, £9, £8, £7 or £6 ... not even a fiver, £4 or £3. In fact, I'm going to make it so cheap you'll hardly know you've bought it. . . . '

In the event, each customer was offered a total of £30-worth of pens for £2.99. His sustained story, vivid demonstration and fabulous endorsement (House of Fraser), combined with irresistible downward price manipulation, proved a sell-out success.

Break up copy—and save your reader getting out of breath
Writing is put into paragraphs for the same reason that we chop up our food before putting it into our mouths: a steak is harder to eat whole; and writing is harder to digest without paragraphs. Look at this slab of writing:

> These are some of the antiques you could consider for a mail-order operation: writing implements, beer mats and labels, advertising ephemera, medals and badges, beer cans, model cars, comics and story papers, corkscrews, fans, old photographs, stocks and shares. There are many others; but a look at why these might be suitable candidates for postal selling will be instructive. None of the suggested mail-order items, apart, possibly, from model cars and photographs, is as yet ripe for faking; simply because it would be cheaper to buy the genuine article than to pay the faker! All of these are small items, either flat, as with comics and ephemera, or easy to pack as a neat parcel: even the biggest corkscrew will fit inside a shoe box.

You must have felt that there were at least a couple of points at which one group of ideas ends and another starts. Such as between '. . . will be instructive.' and 'None of the suggested . . .'. And also between '. . . pay the faker!' and 'All of these are small . . .'.

Now see how much easier it reads with paragraphs.

> These are some of the antiques you could consider for

a mail-order operation: writing implements, beer mats and labels, advertising ephemera, medals and badges, beer cans, model cars, comics and story papers, corkscrews, fans, old photographs, stocks and shares. There are many others; but a look at why these might be suitable candidates for postal selling will be instructive.

None of the suggested mail-order items, apart, possibly, from model cars and photgraphs, is as yet ripe for faking; simply because it would be cheaper to buy the genuine article than to pay the faker!

All of these are small items, either flat, as with comics and ephemera, or easy to pack as a neat parcel: even the biggest corkscrew will fit inside a shoe box.

A new paragraph is a signal to the reader that the next sentence starts a different, though possibly related, set of ideas. It also gives a chance to pause, to let your previous thoughts sink in.

How to make your writing flow
It is possible to understand and have learnt all the elements of good business writing, to have studied models of effective writing, and still be unable to 'write like that'.

One of the greatest steps forward comes when you understand the technique of tying ideas together. This is what makes your writing *move* and draws the readers on, without them even noticing how it is done. If your copy is interesting to boot, it suddenly becomes 'unputdownable'.

There are many types of connective. Nice casual ones, the sort we use in everyday speech, such as 'what's more', 'in any case', 'so', 'on the other hand'. And more formal connectives that are more often used in writing, such as, 'in addition', 'consequently', 'as a result of which', 'appropriately', and many more.

Look at the following piece of copy I wrote to advertise PNA's new computerized media directory.

MAIN TITLE. Stuffed with benefits PR readers will relate to.	*HOW PNA CAN ENSURE THAT YOUR PRESS RELEASES REACH ALL THE RIGHT PEOPLE EVERY TIME, ON TIME.*
SUB-TITLE. Reiterates theme of main title.	Introducing 'PNA *MediaLink*'—the most **up-to-date** and **comprehensive** directory of media **contacts** in the UK.
BODY COPY. Repeats subject of sale, media directory. Dots 'tease' reader on to get to the resolution, 'why'. 'With the result that' harks back to previous sentence, and carries train of thought on. Teasing dots.	Being in the PR business, you've probably come across quite a few **media directories. And** you've no doubt wondered ... **why** is it that Press and other media are not included between the same covers? (**With the result that** you must chase around in other books for radio and TV contacts) ... how is it that they are always so out of date? ... Why do these so-called 'hand books' make you feel as if you were in Hampton Court?...
Refers back to all previous paragraphs.	**If this** has been your experience, then the message contained on this page will be a joyous one for you. **Because** PNA *MediaLink* is the answer to all your prayers for a media reference book worthy of the description it has earned in the trade as the PR's 'bible'.
Lists, if short, virtually guarantee continuity of attention. Second point made.	**First of all,** PNA *MediaLink* is **complete. Press, radio and TV editors, correspondents, producers, are all present** and correct—along with a good number of other, notably City, contacts (of which, more later). **In addition,** PNA *MediaLink* is **up to date.** Media changes are fed into the PNA Media Databank **on a daily basis,** and a fully revised edition of PNA *MediaLink* is delivered to you (by hand in London) every two months....

25

What you see is a liberal use of connectives between paragraphs and also between sentences. In the last paragraph I state that *MediaLink* is 'complete'. The next sentence picks up this point and elaborates on it 'Press, radio and TV editors, correspondents, producers, are *all present and correct*'.

In the next sentence I talk about *MediaLink* being 'up to date'. The sentence that follows echoes this message: 'Media changes are fed into the PNA Media Databank *on a daily basis*.'

Learn how to weld your own copy together using these techniques.

Connectives can colour your copy

The way you join your sentences and paragraphs reveals an awful lot about the tone of your remarks. If you were face to face with a client and you said:

> Our company is very successful. All the executives drive company Minis.

Your client would be able to tell, from your inflexion, your face, even your body language, whether you were being straight or sardonic, trying to impress, and so on. If that person were not there 'in the flesh', but reading a letter from you stating this same fact, you could help him or her to understand, and show how your remarks should be taken, by adding a *connective*:

> Our company is very successful. *In fact*, all the executives drive company Minis.

This would suggest to your reader that you are quite pleased with this state of affairs. If, however, you wrote:

> Our company is very successful. *Nevertheless*, all the executives drive company Minis,

it would be plain that you find this a surprising state of affairs, the Mini being a low-price, downmarket vehicle.

How they filmed the lesbian lovers

THE FULL intended script of Haringey Council's lesbian video for schools can be revealed today.

It involves a writer, a musician, two eccentric tea-ladies and extras.

Left-wing Haringey has give £1685 of ratepayers' cash to a new organisation called Scenic Productions, of West Green Road, Tottenham.

Six women will be involved with the actual filming and they say they want to show that homosexuality is not due "to a cause or reason but arises from a literal choice."

The aim of the video, they say, is to show "a relationship between two women encom-

by Dick Murray

passing issues which the audience can understand."

A Haringey Council report says the video, details of which were revealed in later editions of yesterday's London Evening Standard, will be made in close co-operation with the borough's lesbian and gay unit and could be used "as an educational tool in conjunction with the education services."

Behaviour

Critics of the script say it is "full of innuendo" although explicit sex scenes are not scheduled to be included.

The tale is set in Alexandra

Park and a Tottenham tea rooms—and is divided into seven scenes.

A script supplied to the council says the opening shots will show the writer, driving through the park in her car, having to brake sharply when the musician riding a bike go on their ways annoyed.

Scene two, and the writer is alone in her flat. The script says: "The scene develops her character and shows her everyday efforts and lifestyle."

The script continues with the following scene: "A musician is sat (sic) reading in a teashop. The writer enters and sits opposite. Neither one notices the other one until she sits opposite. Neither one

notices the other one until she sits down. Then they realise how they met.

"The behaviour of two eccentric women, which is very comical, distracts them from their conflict and results in them parting on good terms."

In later sequences the writer's car has stalled—and the musician, cycling by stops to give it a push. The car starts and the musician is given a lift home, with the writer going on her own way.

Later the musician is seen practising the saxophone at home. Meanwhile, the writer at her flat decided to spend the evening indoors and tells her boyfriend on the telephone she is not going out.

Promise

She begins to wonder about a bar the musician has mentioned and gradually builds up courage to go.

The script details the close: "She enters the bar. We see her fears and expectations. The musicians sees her. She is very surprised and pleased.

"The scene ends on a high note with them about to have a conversation.

Mr Ron Bell, Tory opposition councillor on the community service committee which agreed the cash, said today: "It is so full of innuendo and horrific promise that I dread to think how the finished article will end up."

Figure 2.1 This is how a popular newspaper, *The London Evening Standard*, uses cross-heads to break up slabs of copy. Ideally the chosen word or words are sufficiently powerful to tease the reader into reading on. The most skilled copywriters, such as David Ogilvy, devise cross-heads that summarize and telegraph the sales message. That way even if the readers don't read all your sales story they will still get the thrust of your spiel . . . from the cross-heads.

So you see the power of connectives to relate ideas and to give your writing the appropriate weight and 'flavour'.

Cross-heads

Cross-heads are the diminutive titles writers and designers use to break up slabs of type. Usually a cross-head is just a couple of words long, or even a single word, as in the example from *The London Evening Standard* (see Figure 2.1). The words are designed to tease the reader with, here, the promise of salacious bits of story still to come. The

27

'rule' in newspaper offices is that the word or words used in a cross-head should be found no further away than two or three paragraphs. As copy sometimes gets cut in an editing panic, last thing at night, and cross-heads sometimes don't, this can lead to some funny situations, as you will appreciate.

Designers tend to use cross-heads purely as 'breakers', to break up the text. Advertising copywriters who know what they are doing, such as David Ogilvy, use them rather more intelligently and conscientiously. He suggests using them in advertising in such a way that a reader who merely scans the page, but doesn't bother to read all the copy, will still get the 'author's message'.

Take a look at his advertisement for Rolls-Royce entitled 'Should every corporation buy its president a Rolls-Royce?'

> There is much to be said for it. It is a prudent investment. It enhances the public image of the company. And rank is entitled to its rewards.

(Lovely stuff, eh?) Ogilvy specifies *six* cross-heads: 'Longest guarantee', 'No "planned obsolescence"', 'Your president will live longer', 'A *safe* car', 'Free from exhibitionism', 'A source of contentment'.

The thrust of his argument is taken in almost at a glance. Now how will you view cross-heads? As a design device? Or as words worth working at?

Doing it in house style

Almost every newspaper office and publishing house has its own style book. When I worked as a sub-editor on *The Times* we were given a little blue book, which was, as it happens, exactly the same size, colour and shape as the hymn book that bore the crest of my old school. *The Times* style book was meant to be treated with similar reverence.

Long-in-the-tooth subs who had managed to commit

the contents to memory were afforded the kind of respect I imagine cavemen reserved for the elders of the tribe who could recite the history of their people back to the year dot.

Breaking the rules at *The Times* was not exactly a hanging offence, but it lost a few Brownie points. The main aim of having a style book is, of course, consistency. And the more venerable the institution, the more important this may be deemed to be. This early grounding in a rigid house style has, I hope, not cramped my style. But it has made me anxious about breaking, or even bending, rules.

The Times, for instance, decreed that numbers would be written out as one, two, three, etc., up to nine; but thereafter, numerals would be used: 10, 11, etc.

Mindful of the need to be consistent (which also saves thinking time) I tend to follow this rule and other *Times'* stipulations.

But I was recently brought to task by the Director of Operations at The Porchester Group, whose house magazine I produce. 'I don't like all these figures in this conversation,' said Peter George. 'Spell them out.'

I gave him a quick run-down on *Times* style, but he shook his head slowly and grinned. 'I just *know* when it looks right, and this would look better without figures.'

In fact, Peter was not pulling rank. He'd spent 17 years in advertising and publishing and had worked as managing director, with Bamber Gascoigne as chairman, on the revival of the greatest name in 19th century publishing, Ackermann. So Peter knew about words and he appreciated style. But he still trusted his eye most of all. Once you have confidence in yours, I suggest you do the same.

Meanwhile, it may be useful to get hold of a style book, any style book, not necessarily to latch on to its idiosyncracies, but to discover what areas of writing are deemed to be problematic.

The Times for example, was commonsensical about some things. It would put 'Mel Lewis, 43, a writing consultant ...'. Or 'The writing consultant Mel Lewis, 43 years old, ...'. But 'The 43-year-old writing consultant Mel Lewis ...', the hyphens showing that the age specification is used adjectivally.

But there were some quirks at what was then New Printing House Square. The expression 'nonetheless' was always written out as three words: 'none the less'. 'Nevertheless', however, was allowed to be one word.

As you may have guessed, there were a number of cobweb-laden jokes associated with the word 'notwithstanding', which was *not* incidentally written as three words!

Abbreviations are a very good case for showing that house style can be a good thing.

Should you write 'Dr' or 'Dr.'? 'Etc' or 'etc.'? 'No' (short for 'number'), or 'No.'?

The Times had a useful rule of thumb: if the abbreviation ended in the last letter of the unabbreviated word, it omitted the full point. Thus 'Dr', 'Mr', and so on. But 'etc.', short for 'etcetera' should, in *The Times* style, always be followed by a stop: 'etc.'

When 'etc.' is followed by a comma, it has both a stop *and* a comma.

> He had to clean Dad's car, the windows, his shoes, etc., before his Mum would let him go out to play.

My copywriting guru, Lou de Swart, made it a rule never to use the expression 'etc.'—even though people do actually say 'etcetera', and he was always at pains to capture the flavour of popular speech in his work.

Lou maintained that 'etc.' always sounded cheap. He preferred 'and so on'. For some reason, 'and so on' doesn't annoy, even when used heavily; whereas 'etc.' does irritate.

As for 'No', meaning number, you should always write 'No.', simply to avoid confusion with 'No,' the negative. A puzzled reader can quickly turn into an exasperated one. Which can make your copy very put-downable.

3. *Simple, illustrated publicity*

Sometimes it's a puzzle to see just how some people do any business. And when you've worked that out, it then becomes clear that they are certainly not doing anything like as much trade as they could do.

A simple example. Today in the post I got a reminder letter from a couple who have some holiday flats in Cornwall. We had responded, as a family, to an ad the couple had placed last season in one of the 'heavy' Sunday papers, and they were (correctly) prompting us to book their apartment for the up-coming season, even though we had not responded positively first time around.

The slabs of typewritten copy describing the flats had been instant printed and photocopied. The first sentence was a clumsy attempt at flattering the prospective customer that, being demanding, discerning, etc., he would naturally warm to these apartments as being a 'home from home'.

The illustrations of the interiors of the flats, and a view over the harbour, were photocopies of an original colour or black and white print, I could not tell which. The only sensational and eye-catching element in this inept piece of publicity was the price. Close on £400 per flat, for a week in high season.

Now, I presume this couple has, in their property, a saleable commodity. I understand, also, that they need to fill their seasonal schedule, or else why are they writing to me? Most of all, though I puzzle that people who have built in what must be substantial profit margins (even the central heating was an optional extra), have not got the wit to spend some of their booty on professional-looking publicity.

That grouse to one side, you know, as well as I do, that why people *don't* do things in business (or in any sphere of activity) is a perennial imponderable. More is to be learnt by a close study of what people *do* do. Much, therefore, can be gained by understanding how people go about getting the various publicity elements of their business *right*.

Interestingly enough, many, many firms that have no serious advertising budget, still produce some kind of illustrated literature—a brochure, leaflet or similar. Such publicity should always go out with an accompanying, preferably personalized sales letter, reply-paid envelope for response, price list, and so on.

Most firms don't have the funds to carry out market research on any scale. Nor do they need to. Unless new to a market, they already know what they are doing that works, what products sell, which services are in demand, and so on.

Producing a brochure or other kind of simple, illustrated publicity, should, therefore, focus on the following key points:

1. *Aim* What is your publicity meant to accomplish? To win new custom? Induce existing clients to place fresh orders? Or what?
2. *Target audience* The 'universe' for your type of business is the total range of potential customers. One piece of publicity will probably not do for all of them. Which *segment* do you choose?
3. *USP (unique selling proposition)* Why should people buy your goods, commission your services? Flatter yourself: list *all* the reasons. Then pick the one overriding benefit that lifts your business head and shoulders above the competition.
4. *Establish credibility* Business people who handle their own publicity have a tendency to oversell themselves on

paper—even those who would be entirely self-effacing in a face-to-face situation. The aim, to use advertising parlance, is to find the 'believable promise', and then establish credibility.

5. *Winning personality* How you look, speak and behave generally, are all part of your personality. The look, tone and posture of your printed material—is it discreet? Lively but tasteful? Brash and downmarket?—reflects the *personality* of your business. Make sure it is the one you wish to present.

Go window shopping at your worktop

When I used to work as a salesman (salesboy, more like it!) for Brick's and Granditer's menswear stores, the manager, or one of the senior minions, would put on their most unobtrusive face and trek off down the high street to suss out the competition; my uncle the greengrocer did the same; and all of them would adjust their own displays and tickets to take account of the pricing ploys of their rivals.

Most people in business are *au fait* with the actual market-place, but are curiously slow about investigating that other 'shop window' that is even more easily available to them: the brochures and mailings put out by the competition.

Time and again, when I have a brochure assignment it is left to me to dig up comparable material on the market. The client simply hasn't done this elementary homework.

Once you have the competition's brochures, etc., line them up on your desk. Go through the previous points with relation to each of them. What are their aims, target audiences, personality, and so on? If they are already taking a tack you wanted to take, find a way to say it better. There always is a way.

In fact, that's one of the things that has always drawn me to words. My MD clients enthuse about their stock-in-trade, *figures*: 'It's either right or it's wrong', says the figure-crunching MD. How boring! Writing, on the other hand, is infinitely perfectible. Much more interesting!

Research clients, too
Researching your competitors' premises and publicity is relatively easy to accomplish: there are not that many of them, normally. Talking to customers and potential customers, may be trickier. But it will repay you handsomely to research *some* areas of your operation from time to time.

One easy way is to insert a reply-paid card with mailings. Ask about any aspect of your business. Leave a space for 'Any other comments?' You'll be surprised at the results. Even non-clients mailed cold can be co-operative, you'll find, if you give them some inducement to return the card.

To keep their mailing databank up to date, Press release distribution company PNA gets contacts to mail in information on the comings and goings of personnel in the world of journalism and finance by putting the returned cards in a free champagne draw. It works!

Do something different
Make yourself stand out from the pack ... find a benefit, an angle, that the competition is missing. Then spell it out on the cover of your brochure, or in the title of your sales letter, you name it—but say it!

When The Porchester Group, insurance brokers, were sponsoring the Porchester Tyrrell Grand Prix racing car, I wrote a glossy full page ad for them which showed the Porchester-emblazoned car streaking across the page over the headline: 'GOING PLACES?'

We were aiming to capture the attention of that increasingly sought-after sector, the 'upwardly mobile'.

Never overlook the obvious
A lot of people offer publicity services, and many of them

will, of course, do deals on the cost of this service. You can't be inflexible in this kind of business, if you want to stay in business.

But how many bother to say it on their publicity? I did on my broadsheet. I specified a gigantic two-deck heading, with letters an inch deep:

PROFESSIONAL PUBLICITY

AT A PRICE YOU CAN AFFORD

Not only am I prepared to talk, in a relaxed way, about money, the headline suggests, but it hammers home the message that my services are very *reasonable* in any case.

Offer a benefit that matters

Advertising, on behalf of a client, the 'WORLD'S BIGGEST EVER ANTIQUES AND COLLECTORS FAIR', I was looking for some cute angle to pull in last-minute standholders.

We knew from experience that antique dealers like to drive to venues late at night or in the early hours of the morning to avoid traffic.

Then they face the problem of where to camp for the night. Hotels may be closed, full up, too expensive, inconveniently situated, given that bulky goods have to be transported to the site usually at first light, and so on.

Besides which, a lot of dealing is done in the dark, dealer to dealer, even before the show opens and the crowds arrive.

At Wembley Arena, I was able to trumpet:

FREE OVERNIGHT PARKING!

Be believable

After the Wembley antiques fair, we went to town and produced a *Times*-size broadsheet (in fact I called it *TUDOR TIMES*, after the name of the organizers) to tell—and show—everyone what a great event it had been, so they would re-book for the next date.

I used testimonials from delighted standholders, and printed their portraits over the headings, 'RE-BOOKED FOR WEMBLEY' … '9 AM SELLOUT' … 'BOOM IN BELLEEK' (Irish porcelain).

Most important of all, I chose a crowd photograph, taken at the busiest point of the show, and told the designer: 'Make it as big as a TV screen. People believe what they see on telly.'

Set a style, and stick to it

Design is flavour of the month. Designers earn big money, and some are worth it. Companies who can afford to give their products the 'designer touch' can benefit from the instant recognition their goods gain from having a family likeness (see Figures 3.1 and 3.2).

Braun and Philips, the two electrical giants, are examples of companies who have gone overboard on creating a svelte look for items such as electric razors and other personal-care gadgets.

Not every company is able to personalize their wares. Porchester, for example, is a brokerage selling insurance policies, investment plans and so on. They created an eye-catching 'medallion' logo—a castle and a tower with a portcullis, in a circle, in gold—to be the hallmark on all their literature.

Once you've got an identity use it always, on letter-heads, on packs, in ads. Porchester use theirs with wit and originality. On a policy brochure for sportsmen, the cover drawing shows a golf club swinging towards the Porchester logo, balanced on a tee. Porchester's Maritime Plan, a protection policy for divers, oil-rig personnel, and so on, shows the logo bobbing merrily on the waves (see Figure 3.3).

Tell it like it is, but don't tell it all at once

The best advertising headlines contain a *single overriding benefit* or *promise* though the copy may be packed with subsidiary benefits. Brochure material needs a similarly simple approach. Concentrate on one aspect—the biggest, the most popular, the most glamorous, the most dramatic.

Publicity aimed at attracting businesses to Lincoln shows the gorgeous cathedral, not some bleak, modern industrial estate.

If you like it, and it works, stay with it

Having established a workable strategy, an identity, run with them. Freshen-up copy and imagery from time to time, naturally; but stay on the same winning tack.

Be 'newsy'. Failing that, be 'nowsy'

Always announce news, in your writing, if you can. Pitt & Scot, fine art and antiques shipping and packers, discovered a new way to prevent the polished finish of expensive furniture becoming marked in long journeys through hot climates.

I visited the Furniture Industry Research Association in Stevenage; interviewed the scientists who had tested and helped develop the new techniques; I photographed furniture being wrapped in the eight-layer wrapping blanket: I wrote a testimonial from a leading West Coast of America dealer. This low key, specialist item of news became a two-page ad in *Antique Collector* magazine (see Figure 3.4).

The ad was entitled:

MAJOR ADVANCE IN PACKING ANTIQUES

The seven-deck sub-heading continued:

Report on a
new develop-
ment in the
Safe Packing
and Transpor-
tation of Fine
Furniture

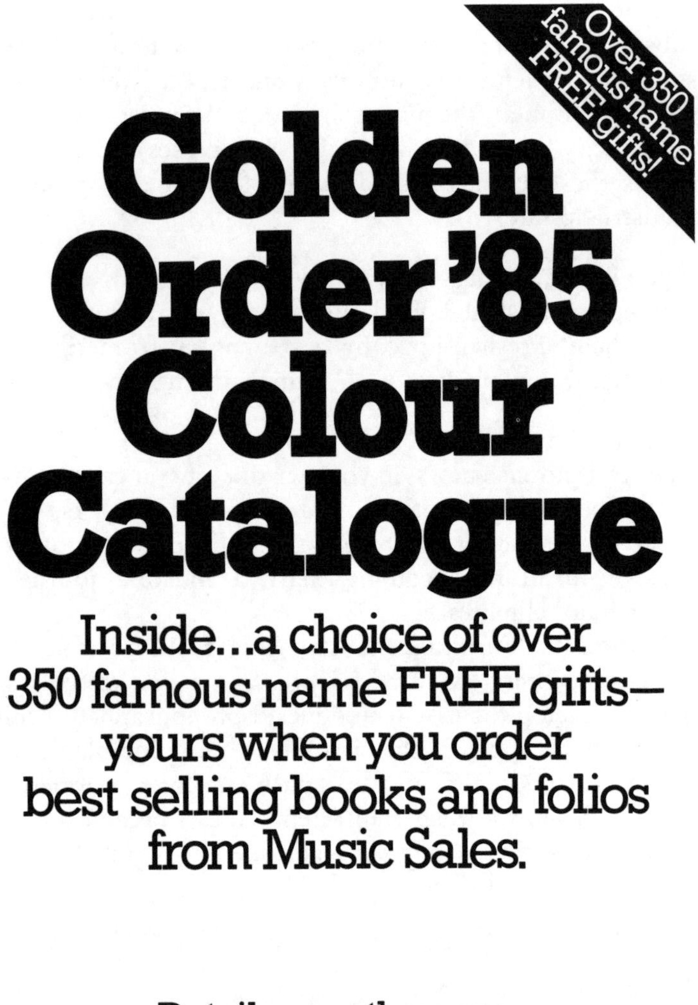
Over 350 famous name FREE gifts!
Golden Order '85 Colour Catalogue
Inside...a choice of over 350 famous name FREE gifts— yours when you order best selling books and folios from Music Sales.
Details over the page.

Figures 3.1 and 3.2 If you can create a 'family likeness' in your publicity material, go for it. 'Familiarity breeds contentment' seems to be the message with this Christmas incentive sales letter and gift catalogue, copy I wrote for Music Sales of America. Another bonus: you can use the same print (black and gold) and type style and save on costs all down the line.

Music Sales Limited
78 Newman Street, London W1P 3LA.
Telephone: 01-636 7777. Telex: 21892.

Golden Order '85

FREE gifts from Music Sales!

Choose from over 350 famous name gifts in the full colour catalogue enclosed with this letter—yours FREE when you use The Golden Order Form.

Dear Dealer,

Don't bother to look for the catch. There is none!

Simply use the Golden Order Form when you place your next order for easy-to-sell publications from the Music Sales Catalogue.

Remember. The more you order, the more FREE gifts you are entitled to.

Last year we offered you "26 gifts of distinction" in the run-up to Christmas. This year, as a special "thank you" for your support throughout 1985, we are boosting that total to more than 350 fabulous famous name gifts. They are all FREE, all yours to choose.

continued overleaf...

Directors: R Wise (USA) Managing, F Johnson, MP Grabham BA ACMA
Registered office: 78 Newman Street, London W1P 3LA.
Registered in England No. 884449.
Distribution Centre:
Music Sales Limited, Newmarket Road, Bury St. Edmunds, Suffolk IP33 3YB.
Telephone: 0284-702600
Telex: 21892

Figure 3.2

Figure 3.3 *The Porchester Maritime Plan*, a specially devised insurance policy offering 'Low-cost cover for people in high risk jobs.... For divers, sailors and other dangerous occupations in the off-shore oil industry' is a product from The Porchester Group, a leading UK insurance broker. I wrote the copy and Director of Operations Peter George art directed the brochure. Once you have established a logo (the golden castle and portcullis of the Group) you don't have to be straightlaced about how you use it. Another Porchester product, for golfers, shows the logo on a tee, pretending to be a golf ball....

40

MAJOR ADVANCE IN PACKING ANTIQUES

by MEL LEWIS

Report on a New Development in the Safe Packing and Transportation of Fine Furniture

Rarely are antiques, arguably the most traditional business in the world, associated with technology and scientific discovery. Yet one company, with a record for reliability and efficiency going back 108 years, consistently breaks this historical rule.

Now Pitt & Scott, acknowledged by the trade to be UK leaders in packing and shipping fine art and antiques, have helped to solve one more problem – a particularly intractable one – connected with the transportation of fine and antique furniture. The problem, stated simply, is that when some antique furniture is shipped overseas, and travels through severe continental changes in temperature, in close confinement in steel containers, the packing material can mark the polished surface of the furniture.

The solution was achieved with the most advanced equipment, in laboratory conditions, using rigorous scientific monitoring techniques.

Although the adverse packing effect is rare – in the experience of Pitt & Scott, better than 90 per cent of antiques shipped through even harsh climates arrives unblemished – nevertheless, where present, the flaw in an otherwise highly creditable record of service, can involve the antiques dealer in costly and time-consuming repolishing, when his main concern is to sell on quickly to secure his planned-for profit.

From Saudi Arabia to the Turner Exhibition

In addition to transporting antiques for dealers, Pitt & Scott are increasingly involved with handling museum acquisitions and domestic and official removal for refurbishment on a grand scale.

When the Saudi royal family chose to re-equip its palace at Riyadh with 200 tables, 134 beds and 160 settees, Pitt & Scott chartered eleven Boeing 707's to meet that task.

The firm also handles loans for many important international art exhibitions. This has involved the transportation, by airfreight, of 27 tons of Henry Moore sculpture (1982/83), and the movement by road, of a sizeable portion of the nation's wealth of Turner paintings to and from Paris in temperature-controlled vehicles (1983/84).

The challenge, then, for the company, was quickly to uprate its already highly regarded service; "Our aim was to improve our packing and eliminate the slight risk of marking, but at nil extra cost to our customers," said Pitt & Scott director George Scott.

After a period of study, Mr. Scott defined the problem as follows: Some polished surfaces are vulnerable when wrapped with traditional paper blanket materials, which can leave a regular pattern of marks under heat and pressure.

Given the firm's long standing in the transportation of precious cargoes, there was no shortage of expertise at hand to tackle the problem: Experimentation at the firm's headquarters in Eden Grove, London N7, could have been followed by a trial shipment. However, this would have

involved a long, uncertain process, packing goods for shipment and then awaiting their return from a long, hot journey.

Clearly no scientific observer worth his salt would let even trusted colleagues at the overseas destination evaluate results. So the goods would need to be returned to England. The resulting double journey would itself have been untypically arduous for valuable antiques.

First Step Towards a Scientific Solution

There had to be another safer, quicker, yet scientifically valid, modus operandi.

Mr. Scott decided to approach the Furniture Industry Research Association * at Stevenage, Herts, an

George Scott who decided to approach the Furniture Industry Research Association

which was to intrigue and occupy the Association through a number of studies over a period of weeks. In the event, their experimentation, in close collaboration with Pitt & Scott, resulted in a successful outcome and a significant advance in packing technique. As a result, almost immediately the company was able to improve its service to the antiques trade.

The Furniture Industry Research Association at Stevenage, Herts.

organisation devoted to the interests of the furniture industry and renowned for the quality and independence of its test findings.

FIRA's normal brief is rather different. They work, usually with modern furniture, testing adhesives, jointing methods, rigid structural materials, as well as upholstery. A FIRA test is characteristically severe, sometimes pursued to destruction, or it

involves working to British Standard Specifications.

Here was a new and subtle challenge for FIRA, one

FIRA's Patrick E. Hughes with the laboratory equipment used in the tests

REPRINTED FROM **THE ANTIQUE COLLECTOR** MAY 1984

Figure 3.4 This 'advertorial'—an advertisement that looks and reads like editorial—first appeared as two facing pages in the magazine *Antique Collector*. Pitt & Scott, sponsors of the ad, took advantage of the magazine printing and ordered a number of extra pages, with the copy printed on two sides of one sheet. This then became part of a publicity pack for general distribution to the Press, potential clients, and so on. In the self promotion business it always pays to think economically—and long.

It was then run off as a two-side insert to accompany all the firm's sales and prestige literature and distributed at the top-rung Grosvenor House Hotel Antiques Fair. From little acorns . . . .

I expect you're wondering about 'nowsy'. Very simple. When the word 'new' is inappropriate, replace it with 'now'. I wrote a Press release for The Porchester Group to win wider appreciation of an already established product. It began

'*Now* from Porchester . . .'

Never be afraid of long copy
'The more you tell, the more you sell' is usually true. Once you pull a reader in past your headline or opening sentence, he is hungry for information . . . entertainment . . . benefits ('What's in it for me?'). The more pricey the product, the harder your words must work and the more of them you may need to clinch the sale or effect the desired response—fill in a coupon, lift the phone, and so on.

Always caption pictures
People like pictures—we know this from television, the numerous Sunday papers that would not be in the running if they did not come complete with colour supplements, the overflowing racks of magazines at the newsagent, and so on.

Pictures are easy to take in and enjoy, an effortless way of absorbing information; stimulating, too. But they also whet a person's insatiable curiosity to know *more* about the subject of the picture: when did you last see a TV documentary that had no words?

Depending on which authority you turn to, readership of picture captions is between two and five times higher than that of body copy. Yet still we see pictures with no caption or only scant wording.

One of the illustrations on my self-publicity broadsheet

shows a spread from a brochure puffing the restaurant and conference facilities of a smart restaurant. The caption reads:

> Elegant colour brochure for The Roof Gardens Restaurant in a spectacular setting on top of the former Derry & Toms building (now the Rainbow Room exhibition centre) in Kensington High Street.

What a pity my illustration was only black and white!

Beware of 'over the top' copy lines
Two firms marketing mail order lists produced brochures advertising their services (see Figure 3.5). One headlines their brochure:

> WE CAN GET YOU THROUGH THE DOORS OF OVER 1 MILLION CUSTOMERS.

The other says:

> FIVE STEPS TO MORE PROFITABLE LISTS
> One complete service from Direct Marketing's leading computer bureau.

The first is clever, clever—the illustration shows a door, and the headline, on a letter, is being posted. It *oversells*. Most companies haven't got a product line that could appeal to a million folk; they're not in a mass-market business. And more, the people behind the doors aren't *customers*, not by a long mail shot: they are merely punters or prospects, depending on your line of trade and the friends you keep.

Start your sales pitch on the cover
Research has shown that four in five people don't progress past the cover of a brochure. So you had better grab your prospect quick with a riveting headline containing a powerful motivating benefit.

I once had to convince a client that this was the way to

43

Five Steps to More Profitable Lists

One complete service from Direct Marketing's leading computer bureau.

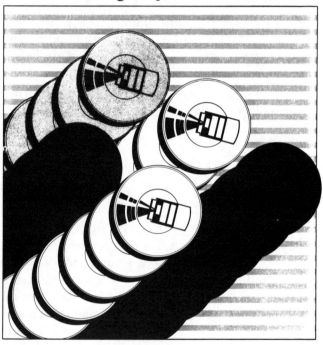

Figure 3.5 Southwark Computer Services produced this simple but compelling brochure. It doesn't offer the world, but contains a *believable* promise: 'more profitable lists'. Nor does it trumpet 'instant success' but a reasonably accessible route to achieving this desirable goal—in 'five steps'.

do a cover. I told him, 'Suppose a man were trying to give away five pound notes in Oxford Circus. What response would he get if he trotted up to people, and said, "Excuse me ...". He'd have trouble getting anyone's ear. In fact, he'd probably land himself a thick one soon enough!'

The client agreed. 'Now suppose he spelled out his message a little more explicitly', I went on. 'He now says, "Excuse me, I'm giving away five pound notes!" He'd quickly have an audience. Agreed?'

The client nodded. 'If this nutcase then decides to produce a handful of notes, and waves them under the nose of the passer-by he'd have an even more dramatic impact on the West End hurley-burley. He might even succeed in giving away some fivers!'

I then explained to the client that the sales talk of our fivers' man is the equivalent of a heading that spells out the sales message. The notes he flashes are a picture that telegraphs that same message. The one supports the other.

In brief, when you write your headline do a stand-up selling job with words. It may be your last chance. And if you use an illustration, choose one that underscores the selling message.

First impressions count

You know it, I know it. But it seems to get forgotten when words are the commodity in question.

One of the more zany tricks I play on my writing students is to roll up with three different briefcases. One is a large doctor's style bag. It looks neat enough, but it's brown and plastic. The other is more of a folio style, something a music student might tote. This is black leather, but worn at the edges.

The third is a Trussardi black leather confection, saddle bag style with monogrammed leather medallion. It cost £220 at Fortnum & Mason.

'Which would you take when going to see a commissioning editor or a client?' I ask them. 'The last one', they chorus. Obviously! It bespeaks success; like which, nothing succeeds.

Even if your budget can't run to full colour and gloss paper inside your brochure, spend a little to give at least the *cover* that quality look.

If something is worth saying once say it again. And again. And again

You must have heard that hoary old story about the man who stands up to make a speech and tells his audience, 'First I'm going to tell you what I'm going to tell you. Then I'm going to tell it to you. And then I'm going to tell you what I told you.'

That's the gist of it. The reality could be something like this—I quote from the Music Sales of America booklet, *Ideas That Sell Music*:

> Most important, none of these ideas will make a hole in your budget pocket. They are easy to put into operation at very low cost.

The second sentence also adds the information that the ideas are *easy* to try (see Figure 3.6). And again from that booklet:

> The ideas ... have been tried and tested. They have worked well for others and they can work for you.

Be positive

Lou de Swart the late, great resident copywriter with Music Sales of America penned that booklet to help the company's team of UK dealers sell more books—-Music Sales of America's song and music books, naturally. He could have called it *Ideas That Help to Sell Music*. Instead he insisted on:

Ideas That Sell Music

Ideas that sell music

The music dealer's do-it-yourself guide to bigger sales.

Figure 3.6 Marred only by the lugubrious illustration, this booklet—a sales aid offered free to franchised and owned music book dealers by Music Sales of America—was written, and titled, by the late great copywriter Lou de Swart. This is what a 'copy-led' production looks like. Lou was mainly of the opinion that a well-chosen word was worth a thousand pictures.

If you've got something that works, don't be afraid to say so.

Give your writing the common touch
People take liberties with grammar, so follow their lead: they'll relate to your copy, it'll be like hearing from a friend. Even when the news is bad . . . .
The Government information leaflet on AIDS says:

> This leaflet is being sent to every household in the country to inform everyone about AIDS, in order to help stop the spread of this serious disease . . .

It should read 'help to stop'. But so what. What's an incomplete infinitive when there are people dying out there?

Positioning
Put simply, you should establish your service or product in the mind of the consumer in a particular way. Approaching this problem in an intelligent, analytical manner, gives you a *strategy*—and may, as a matter of course, put you streets ahead of the opposition who don't think, plan and structure their publicity work in this fashion.

To see positioning in action, take a look at two distinctive, and distinctly different, brochures. Both are for furniture, but there the similarity ends. The first, from Dragons of Walton Street, London SW3, depicts a range of hand-painted furniture for the nursery. The second is a catalogue of fine English furniture in period styles, built by Martin J. Dodge of Bath.

Dragons
1. *Aim* To show some of the range of hand-painted furniture. To sell stock lines 'off the page'. And also to describe the bespoke facility, to draw clients into the shop to place orders.
2. *Target audience* Up-market, stylish parents, keen to

create a pretty, pleasant nursery room that is also unique. And gift buyers, similarly minded.

3. *USP* Deceptively simple, the furniture is actually painted by hand. The chests, beds, and so on (and also soft furnishings) can be personalized with the child's initials, birth date, and so on.

4. *Establish credibility* I used the word 'exclusive' on the cover ('Exclusive hand-painted furniture' is the title) to build up the benefit (See Figure 3.7).

I established the tradition of hand painting ('Painted furniture . . .—a colourful past . . . an even brighter future') by telling the story of painted furniture:

> THE STORY of painted furniture is a rich and fascinating one . . . . The folk art tradition—especially well developed in Scandinavia and The Netherlands—gave rise to quite spectacular and beautiful furniture and room decoration, painting inspired by local flowers, ferns and wildlife . . . . Less well known, however, is the place painted furniture enjoyed in a religious context. The psalter of Eadwine produced in Canterbury in the Middle Ages and now in Trinity College, Cambridge, shows the scribe happily ensconced in a gold, red, blue and green decorated chair . . . .
>
> The great domestic furniture makers were similarly taken with colour. Sheraton . . . enlivened the elegant chairs depicted in his famous *Drawing Room Book* with bright bouquets of flowers and foliage. Everyone was agreed: painting furniture cheered it up: gave it warmth and life. And even simple things—like a chest or a desk—could be made more interesting, more alive.

I explained the breadth of choice: 21 artists to choose, and sought to justify any perceived price premium, by emphasizing value. Hence my closing paragraph:

Exclusive handpainted furniture

Dragons of Walton Street Ltd
23 Walton Street, London SW3
Telephone 01-589 3795/0548

Figure 3.7 This brochure had a number of jobs to do. It was meant to introduce the little known area of painted furniture— which I did by tracing the story (never boring 'history') of rustic hand decoration; to sell off the page via mail order; and establish a cachet for these rather special 'bespoke' items.

One last thought. We are not in the business of reproducing antiques so some of our pieces are adapted from classical designs. But where most new furniture drops in value the second it leaves the showroom, the freshness and sheer personality of hand-painted furniture endures, and this must reflect in value as the years go by.

The back page, a prime selling space so often overlooked, we reserved for praise from the Press and a useful map to enable customers to find Dragons in the labyrinth of streets behind Harrods.

5. *Personality* The brochure (12 pages stapled, with a rear flap to hold price list, order forms, etc.) was four-colour printed on art paper. The aim was to recreate the look of a pretty nursery—each page shows furniture and text on a different pastel-coloured background. In fact, it is a book so appealing a child would be happy to look through it.

The catalogue of Martin J. Dodge (not one of my assignments) came to my attention while I was researching an article on the reproduction antique furniture business. The catalogue caught my eye on a number of counts.

There is very little copy, not much more than the introductory letter from the company's founder, Martin J. Dodge. Instead, the brilliantly photographed furniture and room settings do the job of describing and selling remarkably well on their own, with minimal captioning.

This is a top-of-the-tree product range, and the company image reflects this status.

1. *Aim* The MD spells it out:

This catalogue covers the most comprehensive collection of fine English furniture that we have ever manufactured.

Customers are invited to study the catalogue at home

before visiting the firm's five splendid showrooms in Broad Street, Bath.

2. *Target audience* Homemakers, those with some antique pieces, seeking furniture of complementary taste and quality (the company also copies customers' antiques, to complete a depleted set of chairs, for example); companies furnishing boardrooms, conference rooms; embassies needing furbishment; and so on.

3. *USP* Martin has a simple enough credo:

> Martin Dodge, a third generation cabinet maker and master craftsman, founded his business in 1968 with the single aim of making available the finest in English furniture.
>
> His designs and skills follow in the best tradition of the 17th and 18th century designers such as Chippendale, Adam, Hepplewhite and Sheraton.

There is no artificial ageing of the pieces: the furniture is intended to stand on its own merits as new pieces 'in the style of' the cabinet-making greats.

4. *Establish credibility* You must have heard the phrase 'the medium is the message'. This applies as much to printed publicity as any other medium. Produce a flimsy, badly printed, scruffily thought-out piece of publicity, and this must rub off on the consumer's perception of the products depicted—however good they may be in reality.

The catalogue of Martin J. Dodge bespeaks quality and good taste. The designer uses Astrolux (shiny, heavy art paper) for the cover, and square binding (the spine has a flat edge to it, like glossy magazines of the ilk of *Vogue*, *Country Life*, and so on). The cover is green with gold lettering, as elegant as anything put out by Harrods.

In fact, to underline that one must pay for quality, the catalogue is not given away, but sold for a few pounds, refundable on purchase of goods over a certain figure.

5. *Personality*   Decidely up-market in quality and style, yet there is something curiously approachable about this piece of publicity, revealed in two simple ways.

The first is the elegant, black and white line drawing that extends to two pages as a frontispiece to the catalogue. It shows a tantalizing view of Bath (The Royal Crescent), and clearly the firm is at pains to establish proximity to, and sympathy with, such elegance, breeding, etc.

Then there is the photograph of 'our sponsor'. The picture shows not some stuffy chap, uncomfortable in his Sunday best against a studio backdrop, but Mr Dodge, in sweater and open-necked shirt, sitting at his desk *hard at work*.

To emphasize the lack of pose, he is looking down at some paperwork, not at the reader, and we view him in profile.

To my way of thinking, the personality of this man shines through. He knows the worth of his work and prefers to let it speak for itself, through the photographs and the simple good taste of the design of the catalogue, which succeeds in being something of a masterpiece of *understatement*.

Newsletters

Be newsy in your business writing is sound advice. A person in business loves reading about anything new. It arouses curiosity and at the back of the mind there is the suspicion that some new product, system or technique could actually help make more money or improve the company's operation. One of the easiest ways to tap into this reflex, is to produce a *newsletter*. Newsletters can be simple one or two-siders, a folded double-size A4 size, printed all four sides, or any larger size (See Figure 3.8.). I am a fan of the broadsheet, a one or two-sider as big as *The Times* or *The Independent*, and other 'heavy' dailies.

I love the scale, the opportunity to use really bold head-

Figure 3.8 This is my personal publicity. It started life as a one-sider advertising the range of 'off-the-shelf' articles available through my agency, Editor's Choice Features Service. My experience on *The Times* and other broadsheets convinced me that the large format has instant status and impact. Using the flip side to sell my publicity services was clearly a cost-effective move.

55

REMARKABLE NEW SYSTEM HELPS BUSY PRs DO MORE AND BETTER BUSINESS

Suppose the whole business of writing, targeting and distributing Press releases could be made simpler, quicker, more cost effective . . . and the means of achieving these time and money-saving benefits were available to you now. Wouldn't it make sense to find out more about such an advantageous system?

Indeed it would. Especially as such a system has in fact been developed and is available to you *immediately* and at *remarkably low cost.*

PR Targeter, as the system is known, is a computer-based "tool" of the trade designed specifically for the professional PR executive. As such, it is capable of transforming the working life of a busy PR person, like yourself, resulting in cost savings which will more than offset the low establishment cost and the system's even more modest upkeep.

PR Targeter is a complete desk-top media and communications system, incorporating Telex, electronic mail, media databank, automatic telephone management, and more. It is based on a desk-top computer (similar to the one you probably already own, and which may even be suitable for use with PR Targeter — so saving still more in initial outlay), and a unique software program, which carries virtually all of the information contained in PNA's comprehensive databank of UK Press, radio and TV contacts. You are already familiar with this information in its printed version as *PR Planner* and *PNA MediaLink.*

As Easy As Paging The Oracle

PR Targeter puts all of this information at your fingertips, on screen, at the touch of a button. And more, it enables you to transmit this information at will. To your client, for approval, or to PNA, for printing and sending out your release.

Scanning the media lists, selecting your mailing options — including your own private and "bespoke" lists, which can also be programmed in — is a swift and painless activity. As easy, in fact, as paging the Oracle!

Then key in your Press release and word process it to perfection. If you want to study previous releases, you can summon them from PR Targeter's prodigious memory. You can print "hard" copy to re-work on the train, take home,

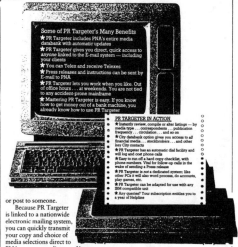

Some of PR Targeter's Many Benefits
★ PR Targeter includes PNA's entire media databank with *automatic* updates
★ PR Targeter gives you direct, quick access to *anyone* linked to the E-mail system — including your clients
★ You can Telex and receive Telexes
★ Press releases and instructions can be sent by E-mail to PNA
★ PR Targeter lets you work when you like. Out of office hours . . . at weekends. You are not tied to any accident-prone mainframe
★ Mastering PR Targeter is easy. If you know how to get money out of a bank machine, you already know how to use PR Targeter

PR TARGETER IN ACTION
★ Instantly review, compile or alter listings — by media type . . . correspondents . . . publication frequency . . . circulation . . . and so on
★ City databank option gives you access to all financial media . . . stockbrokers . . . and other key City contacts
★ PR Targeter has an automatic dial facility and will log and cost phone calls
★ Easy to run off a hard copy checklist, with phone numbers. Vital for follow-up calls in the wake of sending a Press release
★ PR Targeter is not a dedicated system; like other PCs it will also word process, do accounts, play games, etc.
★ PR Targeter can be adapted for use with any IBM compatible unit
★ Any queries? Your subscription entitles you to a year of Helpline

or post to someone.

Because PR Targeter is linked to a nationwide electronic mailing system, you can quickly transmit your copy and choice of media selections direct to PNA . . . to your client . . . You can even send a copy of your release electronically to Press clippings agency Romeike & Curtice. Or you can opt to print out your own gummed labels.

Whatever course you choose, you must save time. And if you decide to use PNA's printing and distribution services (which includes hourly hand deliveries to the major media and the City), you can achieve all of your objectives without leaving the desk or talking on the phone.

In fact the only demands on you are your brainpower and a little fingerwalking over some keys.

The Bottom Line

PR Targeter, complete with media databank, Telex, electronic mail, modem, all software, labelling system and databank updating, is £1510 (plus VAT, with a 10 per cent discount to IPR and PRCA members); renewal cost is currently £389 per annum. Suitable microcomputer equipment to use with PR Targeter is available, from £1,000.

continued overleaf

Figure 3.9 I write and produce the *PNA Newsletter*, which appears every two months and is circulated free to clients of the company's Press distribution and media information service. The publication has been useful in establishing PNA's hi-tech innovation, *PR Targeter*, a unique software package that turns a desk-top personal computer into a complete media selection and command centre. PR executives are able to summon media information, select their mailing targets, word-process their Press releases, then transmit this information by electronic mail.

56

lines and photographs as big as a place mat. Also, of course, the more your newsletter looks like a newspaper, the more the reader is apprised of its aim: to impart *news*.

The classic newsletter, however, carries no illustrations and certainly no advertising. I refuse to be bound by these 'rules'. If you can persuade clients and others to advertise, why not do it and offset your costs? Then, of course, you may find yourself having to give them 'advertorial' as part of the package—but that's another matter.

Your newsletter should go to your client base, obviously. And also to potential clients, suppliers, and so on.

The biggest mistake companies make is using their newsletter as an excuse to puff themselves—their achievements, acquisition of new clients, etc. There is a place for this. But never overlook the fact that your readers are much more interested in *themselves* than in you.

That's why in writing the *PNA Newsletter* (Figure 39), aimed at PR professionals, I included an article entitled 'HOW TO WRITE PRESS RELEASES THAT REALLY HIT THE SPOT'.

To get my material, I went straight to the horses' mouths. I interviewed the news editors of *Today*, the *Daily Express*, *The Guardian* and other nationals. The designer used the papers' logos to telegraph the message that this was 'the real thing'. I understand the article had a high readership.

4. *Better letter writing*

The letters you send out from your business can do a big job for you. They can bring you more orders, or keep your customers happy; they can collect money for you more easily, or make people glad they are dealing with you. A letter, in short, is powerful ammunition in the business of doing business.

If you want to write successful letters and always achieve your object—there is only one way. You have to work at it. You don't need a degree in English. There are plenty of university professors who couldn't write a decent business letter if they tried. And there are plenty of down-to-earth business people and professional copywriters making their letters work for them all along the line.

In my far-from-humble view most British business correspondence is appalling—dull, boring, cliché-ridden. But most of all unfriendly and remote. The Americans are far better letter writers. Here's a typical one. It's both friendly *and* businesslike.

Dear Mr Rickenbacker

A line of credit has been opened in your name, and with it go our very best wishes for a happy and prosperous Easter.

Saying 'hello' to a new retailer is always a happy experience for me. I intend to do everything possible to help you profit from our relationship; and that's not all. I'm confident we will become, more than just your suppliers, but your friend, too.

An easy way to start winning extra income is yours

for the asking—by taking advantage of our substantial discount terms. . . .

The first rule of successful letter writing
KNOW WHAT YOU WANT TO SAY. You'd be surprised how many people sit down to write a letter without any clear idea as to what they are setting out to achieve. Ask any secretary how much time the boss takes 'umming and ahing'.

One way to know what it is you want to say is to write a draft. Or tell someone what you want to say; that also focuses the mind wonderfully. Good letters don't get written, they get rewritten, sometimes several times over. Don't plead lack of time. The truth is, time spent on getting your letters right can be the most profitable you ever spend.

Second rule of successful letter writing
BE CLEAR. If your reader doesn't understand you, you won't get what it is you're after: an order, money owed to you, whatever.

There's a secret to clear writing. It's this: *short words . . . short sentences . . . short paragraphs.* Call that rule 'the three shorts'—and never forget it. Cut the cackle when you write. Silence isn't golden in business; brevity is.

Schoolteachers will tell you never to use several words where one will do. When it comes to successful letter writing, they're wrong. Never use one long word where 10 short ones will do the trick. And don't use 10 short ones if fewer will do.

Common examples? 'I acknowledge receipt of' instead of a homely, 'Thank you for'. 'We are writing with reference to,' instead of the everyday, 'We are writing *about*'. Suppose you were apologizing for a delay. Which do you think sounds better: 'We have received an extremely large volume of orders', or 'We have been snowed under with orders'?

Famous advertising man Arthur Kudner says: 'Big, long words name little things. Big things have little names, *life*, *death*, *hope*, *love*, *peace*, *war*, *home*'. It isn't easy, learning to use little friendly words. But the more you strive at it, the easier it gets and the easier your letters read, the more successful they will become.

One way to get your letters sounding chattier is to 'talk' on to paper. Ask yourself this: what would you say to the people you're writing to if they were in the room? Write it down, rough as you like, and with contractions, like 'I'll' and 'don't'. Then work it over, with a pen, until it reads right. PS, 'talking' letters is also a great way of rolling aside a writer's block!

Now for sentences
Most long sentences are simply a series of short sentences strung together. Very often, these short sentences are joined by words like 'and' or 'but'. If you have written such sentences, it's an easy matter to break them down into shorter ones.

Take this example of a long sentence with long words:

> We acknowledge receipt of your letter of the 18 March and have to inform you that the goods you ordered were not in stock when we first received your order, but you will be pleased to know that they are now available and we will be despatching them today.

You read sentences like that, day in, day out, in business letters. Now look at it rewritten:

> Thanks for your letter of 18 March. When your order first arrived, the goods you wanted were not in stock. But we are glad to tell you that the new stocks are now in, and we are sending your order today.

Avoid long-winded, hackneyed expressions. You would think that by now everyone had seen, or been told about, the section in the magazine *Private Eye* in which readers were asked to send in cuttings (usually from sociological publications) which used that laughably ponderous expression, 'ongoing situation'. Still the words crop up in letters and articles with deadpan seriousness.

At *The Times*, a pet hate of sub-editors was the expression 'in the field of'. To many writers people aren't 'computer scientists', they are 'experts in the field of computer science'.

'At this moment in time' is another phrase that occurs with sickening regularity on television, radio and in newspapers. 'Now' does just as well. Why do people use these tedious catchphrases? I don't know. I think it's because the ability to speak at length, without pausing, is a highly rated skill in Western civilization. Also, it gives conversation an illusion of importance.

Consider ditching all the left-hand expressions that follow, in favour of those on the right:

We acknowledge receipt of	Thank you for
Is not in a position to	Cannot
May rest assured	May be sure
Under separate cover	Separately
Advise us as to	Let us know
The undersigned	I or me
In lieu of	In place of
Pertaining to	About
In the event that	If
At which time	When
It is our understanding that	We understand
Inadvertently	Unintentionally
Along the lines of	About
We are of the opinion that	We believe
In view of the fact	Since
In the near future	Promptly or soon
Ultimo	Of last month
Proximo	Of next month

Give consideration to	Consider
In the amount of	For
We would like you to	Please
With reference to	This or these
The said application	Application
Consensus of opinion	Consensus
In connection with	About
With regard to	Concerning
We are returning herewith	We enclose
Pending receipt of	Until
With respect to	Concerning
Be so kind as to	Will you please
At this moment in time	Now
At the present time	Now

By the way, don't let anyone tell you that it is wrong to start a sentence with 'and' or 'but'. Nothing of the kind. The best business writers do it. You, too, will often find it a handy way to break long sentences down into short ones.

Here is a quote from the lead article in a copy of *The Sunday Times*:

> In Washington, the State Department declined to comment on the threat to the four Americans. But the administration has let it be known that if any hostage is killed action will be taken against those responsible.

(As a matter of interest, I find 'killed action' gives me a knee-jerk reaction, and would certainly have included a comma between those words.) Beginning with 'But' is good enough for these paragons of the Press; and 'and' is good enough for top copywriters, such as those employed by M. P. Brown, Inc, of Burlington, Iowa:

If you will tell me ...
... whether you wish your check protector sent to your office or your home, one will be shipped to you

at once. *And you can use this amazing new machine 10 days free!*

As for short paragraphs, this is by far the easiest aspect to master. Nothing makes a letter more unreadable than big blocks of type. It's the simplest thing in the world to cut off a paragraph after three or, at most, four sentences and start a fresh one. Your letter will look better for it and will be read that much more easily.

How long should your letter be? There is only one answer. As long as is necessary to say what you want to say. If you are asking for an order, tell your reader all the advantages of the goods you are offering. If you are offering a bargain, say so. Never miss a trick in a 'selling' letter, no matter how long it gets. If you want to learn how to write successful letters, study the letters sent out by the most successful letter writers in the world.

Who are they? *Reader's Digest* ... Time-Life ... American Express. Their letters are models of clarity. They never use one word more than necessary—or one word less. Don't let anyone tell you the old story, 'Their letters go straight in the waste-paper basket'. *Reader's Digest*, Time-Life and American Express are among the richest businesses in the world. The first two built their fortunes entirely on subscription-getting letters. The third relies heavily on follow-up letters to its prospects to get more business.

Always *finish* your letter by telling your readers just what it is you want them to do. Or just what it is you are going to do for them. This is the most important part of your letter—the action part (Figure 4.1).

Studies have shown that the parts of a letter that get the closest attention are the first and last paragraphs and the PS. Use that fact to get your own most urgent messages across. Don't be afraid to repeat yourself.

Don't dangle your reader. Never say, 'Please let us have your reply at your convenience'. Say, 'Please reply within

Mel Lewis
Editor-in-Chief
Editor's Choice Features Service

Lewis Associates
2 Dagmar Passage
London N1 2DN
01-359 5749

10 April 1997

Financial and Legal
Correspondent,
Parents magazine

Former Consumer
Correspondent
Femail, Daily Mail

Columnist,
Antique Dealer &
Collector's Guide,
IPC

Antiques columnist
Market Trader

And contributor to
the National Press,
including:
The Times
The Sunday Times
Colour Magazine,
Daily Telegraph
Guardian
Daily Express
Evening Standard
Look Now
She
Men Only
Family Circle
Pix (Australia)

Mel Lewis is the
author of:

*How to Make
Money from
Antiques*
(Blandford)
*Collecting for Fun
and Profit*
(Proteus)
*How to Collect
Money that is
Owed to You*
(McGraw-Hill)

Dear

FREE ARTICLES BY FLEET STREET WRITERS

As you probably know, The Porchester Group, the well known
insurance broking company, is teaming up with Cornhill (sponsors
of Test cricket for many years), to form a new financial services
group.

The exact name and shape of that organisation will be announced
very soon. Meanwhile, one service that Porchester would like
to establish right now, is to offer editors of major provincial
papers, like yourself, the chance to run lively financial articles.

The articles are yours to use free of charge. And they are offered
to you exclusively in your area. But exclusively by response.

In other words, if you respond faster than other editors in your
area your paper will win exclusive area rights.

For as long as you maintain your own interest in the series no
rival paper will get the articles (as far as this is in our power
to monitor).

As you can appreciate, the idea is very new. And articles are
FREE. All that is asked is that the line "Compiled with the
assistance of The Porchester Group" is added at the foot of
each article (or elsewhere).

Porchester has offices in London (City and West End), Birmingham,
Bristol, Liverpool and Manchester · Perhaps you could find the
town appropriate for you --- e.g., --- "The Porchester Group,
Manchester" --- to help readers locate their nearest branch.

I have enclosed two of the most compelling titles: "ALTERNATIVE
INVESTMENT" and "RETIRING? ONE WAY TO GET CASH
FROM YOUR HOME WITHOUT MOVING OUT".

Editor's Choice Features Service
is a Division of Lewis Associates
VAT registration no. 299 3954 84

Mel Lewis
Editor-in-Chief
Editor's Choice Features Service

Lewis Associates
2 Dagmar Passage
London N1 2DN
01-359 5749

- 2 -

These are yours to use once you confirm your interest quickly,
using the enclosed reply-paid envelope and reply form attached
--- and I come back to you to say that you are first in line for
your area.

We are currently adding a new title every week. Naturally we
would prefer you to use the articles on a regular basis --- please
say how frequently you will be able to run the articles, on that
reply form.

To help us give you the best possible service, please circle the
options listed on the folio attached. Then get your secretary
to send it back to me right away, if you will, in the stamped,
self-addressed envelope provided, together with a compliments
slip or letterhead --- no need for a letter.

I will quickly let you know if you are first for your area and
send you all the articles of your choice by return post, first
class.

Clearly, the sooner you get that letter in the post, the more
likely you are to earn the right to use some very readable copy
at a price you cannot afford to miss out on --- nothing.

Yours sincerely

MEL LEWIS

p.s. Please turn to page 11 of the enclosed journal, "Porchester
Live". There is an article by me entitled THE GREAT DIVIDE.
It's all about the new book, HOW TO SPLIT UP AND SURVIVE
FINANCIALLY, written by Tony Hetherington, a Sunday Times
columnist and regular contributor to "Porchester Live!"

The book, his first, is full of good advice to divorced and separated
couples, as well as those simply anxious to know where they
stand. Tony has given permission for you to quote from this
article. Or to use all of it, as you wish. There is no charge,
and no credit to Porchester is required for this article.

Editor's Choice Features Service
is a Division of Lewis Associates
VAT registration no. 299 3954 84

Figure 4.1   This sales letter, penned on behalf of The Porchester Group making use of my features syndication agency, Editor's Choice, was an outrageous success. In a sample mailing of 130 editors from an area 'universe' of about 500, 32 papers replied. Nine papers said they would take the offered financial column on a weekly basis and eight said they would take it at some other frequency. Three more said they could not make immediate use of the offer but asked me to 'keep in touch'. Distribution specialists PNA handled the media targeting and mailing.

the next seven days' or 'by return', or whatever. If it's an order you want, ask your reader to post the order *now*, *today*, *this very moment*. If it is an appointment you are after, suggest the day when you would like to call.

Every letter you send out builds a picture of your business, the quality of your goods, the efficiency of your service. Make sure that picture is the best you can project.

The letter reproduced as Figure 4.2 is remarkable on many counts. Not only is it a model of intriguing, entertaining and personalized prose—by an inspired amateur who has read books on copywriting, mastered every worthwhile technique and is probably a 'natural' anyway—but it also sold me personally on the painting and decorating service being offered. I did not believe that anyone could be so convincing on paper and not actually produce the goods.

And sure enough, the work by Duncan J. MacLean and his colleagues is outstanding. As they say, 'If you've got it, flaunt it!'.

Why are letters rated so highly as a sales medium?
I'll give you one reason right away, one you'll appreciate, being in business—they are cost effective. The rest, which will be revealed in the following pages, will be cream on the trifle.

My 1912 eighth edition of A. W. Shaw & Company's *How To Write Letters That Win* spells it out.

> Used rightly, it is, [the letter] in many respects a better medium than a personal representative. Certainly it has all the advantages in cost. A sales letter entails no heavy travelling expenses, hotel bills and entertainment charges; a penny [sic!] stamp carries it the length of the land. Nor does it cool its heels in the outer office and conjure methods to reach the chief within; the courtesy of the post lays it upon his desk. It

Duncan J. MacLean

Fine Painting & Decorating

61 Lincoln Road, East Finchley N2 9DL   01- 444 6970

Dear Sir/Madam,

I have a number of satisfied customers in this area. You are welcome to look at my work and talk to my customers at:

2, 4, 9, 11 Birchwood Avenue, N10	36, 49 Lanchester Road, N6
10, 48, 50, 47 Princess Road, NW1	28 Park Village East, NW1
1, 12 Clifton Hill, NW8	29 Stanhope Gardens SW7
26, 32 South Hill Park, NW3	5 Wilton Court, SW1
29, 36 Buttermere Court, NW8	20 Buckland Crescent, NW3
1, 3 Courtside, N6	31 Church Crescent, N10
10, 16 Ashburnham Close, N2	10 Milton Park, N6

I have some good old-fashioned decorating habits. First, I wash down paintwork where necessary with sugar soap solution and rinse off. This removes all dirt and grease and leaves a clean sound surface providing a good base for new paint. Then I rub down to a smooth even surface with wet abrasive paper. I apply two undercoats where needed, as on some colour changes and on newly primed work. On new or bare wood I apply knotting solution so that you won't get unslightly blisters three months later. I apply two coats of gloss where warranted to give a deep solid gloss finish to brighten your home and stand up to years of use.

I strip wallpaper with a steam stripper. This is cleaner and faster than other methods. Your carpets won't get soaked. The walls are left clean, sterilised and free from gouges and holes. I crossline (where possible) with a heavy grade lining paper. This provides a flat even surface and excellent adhesion for your chosen finish paper. Lining brings out the best in your paper. I protect your furniture and carpets with clean, frequently washed dust sheets. I clean up as I go and leave your house clean and tidy.

On exterior work I use traditional paints which will last five to ten years and then only require minimal preparation and repainting. Every year I return and wash down and touch up your paint leaving your house clean, bright and free from corrosive dirt. This prolongs the life of your paintwork.

My men are trained and experienced. Some are trained to City and Guilds standard and hold certificates. I provide correction and training to improve the quality of service and the work.

I love kids and can usually keep them out of the paint tins. I stick to my word and my schedule and am generally not a bad chap. Go along and have a look at our work. I will give you a free quotation and advice on your decoration requirements inside or out.

Yours sincerely,

Duncan J. MacLean

Duncan J. MacLean

Figure 4.2   Here's what an inspired amateur sales letter writer can achieve. Duncan has also studied the craft, as you will appreciate. The result is a masterpiece of 'you' copy, a really friendly style, and most of all—given that he is aiming to do *business*—a truly credible testimonial—not a bad thing to establish in the seedy world of cowboy builders and decorators.

follows up persistently when repeated personal calls would be impossible. . . .

Powerful stuff. Just one point in mitigation. These days, the phone may be overtaking the letter as the sales executive's 'flexible friend'.

Consider this. Have you never gone into a store and been served—or rather, *half* served—when the phone rings and the assistant goes off to answer it, and then proceeds to spend more time, more solicitously attending to the caller's needs than yours? You are there in the shop; a solid gold prospect; in a position to hand over hard currency, or at least a piece of plastic, and for some curious reason the caller on the phone makes the running!

Why is this? Why does the sales assistant rarely say to the caller, 'Hold on. I'll be with you in a minute. I have a customer to attend to'? Why is real life (you, in the flesh) so much less important than the disembodied voice on the phone?

Two conclusions to draw. First, from a business point of view, simply accept the fact that the phone *is* a mesmerizingly powerful tool, capable of capturing attention as nothing else, and try to weave an element of telephone selling into your own sales programme.

Second, the very best sales people understand all this and use the phone intelligently to warm up prospects. But they also appreciate that there is nothing like a body for doing business with. When the phone rings, they courteously apologize to the client they are with, answer the 'dog and bone', take a number, and promise to ring back 'very soon'. These realists do even more business.

The book continues 'the good sales letter ... must contain':

1. The opening, which wins the readers attention and prompts him to go farther into the letter.
2. Description and explanation, which gains his interest by picturing the proposition in his mind.

3. Argument or proof, which creates desire for the article you have to sell by showing its value and advantages.
4. Persuasion, which draws the reader to your way of thinking by showing the adaptation of the article to his needs and his need of it now.
5. Inducement, which gives him a particular or extra reason for buying.
6. The climax which makes it easy for the reader to order and prompts him to act at once.

These elements may be taken, in fact not only as the basis of the successful sales letter but of every good business letter. For a collection letter is only a form of salesmanship on paper—you are selling your man a settlement of his account. And a reply to a complaint is but another—you are selling your man satisfaction. Over the whole field of correspondence the same principle applies.

Today, the writing formula outlined above is better known in its condensed form, by the mnemonic 'A.I.D.S.' or 'A.I.D.A.'. The letters stand for Attention, Interest, Desire, Action, or Suggest Action. This simple plan can be used to improve many forms of commercial writing, not just sales letters, but almost every form of business letter and also advertising. Structure your writing like this:

A. Get your reader's attention by pertinent, relevant means. In an ad, this means write an intriguing, benefit-packed headline. Many letters also benefit from headlines. Or write an attention-grabbing opening sentence.

I. Having caught your reader, hold on to him or her by arousing *interest*. Do this by immediate enlargement on the promise of the headline or opening statement. Many business writers blot their copy-writing book by ignoring this fact. They start strong, but in the first paragraph they wander off at a tangent.

Once you've attracted your reader, follow up on the point you've made. Explain your headline in more detail ... expand on the opening sentence. If you are following my advice, the early words will have contained a *benefit*. Enlarge on this benefit.

D. In advertising circles the 'D' stands for *desire*: you must now stimulate desire, strongly enough to prise the prospect from his or her money. I've also seen the 'D' standing in for *demonstrate*—prove that you have the facts to back up the promise of A and I. In other words, bring in your story here, to support your argument.

S. *Show* an effect, *suggest action* on the part of the reader, or *summarize*, depending on the type of writing job in hand.

How to 'rabbit' on in style

Before I wrote about breeding rabbits I knew as much about rabbits as I knew about hares: aren't they both daft as a brush? By the time I'd researched the rabbit meat market, however, I was something of an authority.

But don't blind your readers with science. Besot them with *benefits*. This I proceeded to do.

	Dear Friend
ATTENTION won	Going into rabbit production could well be the wisest business move you ever make. For the hard-working man or woman, money-making opportunities are limitless. The demand for rabbit meat is growing all the time.
	Yet your initial investment is very reasonable: you can get started with low-cost, quick-breeding young rabbits for only a few pounds each.
INTEREST aroused	Very quickly you could build up to a 150-doe unit which would bring in

enough money to help buy a new car ...
go towards the mortgage ... pay for an
exciting long holiday.

And the potential is there for a full-time
200–400 rabbitry. Just imagine: no more
workday blues. No more travelling to
work, to help someone else make profits.
Instead, independence in your own back
yard. Cash in your pocket. No one to
call boss! No one but you, that is!

And getting started is easy

ARGUMENT
begun

You don't need a vast acreage. The mini-
mum area suitable for rabbits is not
large—one cage is around 6 sq. ft. and
you can build one cage on top of another
(with adequate ventilation space and
allowing a 2 ft. path between cages, for
servicing).

Meat rabbits don't eat expensive greens
either; they eat cheap, specially nourish-
ing pellets. So no mess, no costly waste.
And they grow fatter faster. Which
means more money in your pocket.

PERSUASION
pursued

But not any rabbit will do. You must
have carefully bred and selected breeding stock. And this is where XXX
XXXX can help. We sell only the best—
New Zealand Whites. And we are accre-
dited Commercial Rabbit Association
(CRA) breeders.

Read what the CRA say about NZ
Whites: 'The New Zealand White ... is
a pure bred albino and probably the
most popular breed for meat production
at the present time.

Selling your rabbits for meat is easy. Your live rabbits go to a 'packer' who does all the work for you. Or you can work with a local group—see brochure for list of addresses.

ACTION
advised

So you see, it really is easy to start making money in rabbits. Let me hear from you soon. It will be your first step forward in a better business. The sooner you start the better.

Yours sincerely

XXX XXXX

INDUCEMENT
introduced

p.s. See below a typical year's budget per rabbit. It gives a vivid idea of the money you could make. Start now—send your order today.

PROFIT CHART

Typical profit potential for one doe per year, under normal conditions and using one of our New Zealand White breeding stock

---

One doe produces 50×5 lb meat rabbits a year
To reach 5 lb each rabbit will have eaten 5×3 lb feed (food conversion rate: 3 to 1) $= 15$ lb

Feed cost 4.59p per lb $= 69$p

Rabbit sells for meat @ 34p per lb live weight $= £1.70$

Profit over feed per rabbit	= £1.01
50 × 5 lb rabbits offspring per doe per year 50 × £1.01	= £50.50

How your money could grow
50 breeding does yield

50 × £50.50	= £2525
100 breeding does yield	
100 × £50.50	= £5050

and so on.

Note: account should also be taken of cost of electricity, disinfectant, etc.

One of the most demanding types of letter I have to write is where I am touting for business. It really is on a par with selling a product—I'm selling my services. With one important difference. I often go direct to my prospects and talk about their own business, the gist of which is that they are, in my view, not doing as much business as they could be doing—with my help.

This takes tact, humour and a thick skin. Given the odds against such head-on operations being successful my hit rate is surprisingly good.

Here is one letter I sent to the managing director of a printing company. My attention had been caught by a flyer or leaflet the company had sent out trumpeting its new business acquisitions. In lipstick-red felt tip, the headline screamed:

**RESULTS
SPEAK LOUDER THAN
ANY SALES LETTER!**

I disagreed with the sentiment, was queasy about the brashness of the typography, and I decided to chance my arm. I wrote to the managing director:

Dear Mr MD

You may be right. Your recent mailing may have a point. Results may 'speak louder than any sales letter'. But tell me, what evidence do you have that the noisiest salesman also does the most business? And pulls in the most cheques?

Suppose you went into a shop to buy a suit. And the salesman started shouting at you the moment you stepped through the door. He told you what an ace salesman he was ... how many suits he'd sold that month ... how much commission he'd made on them ... and so on.

Would that impress you? Would that make you want to step up to be measured up? To reach for your cheque book?

Or might you be more interested in the suit salesman who stepped up, briskly, cheerfully, and offered to help. Who then went to some trouble to find out what you were really looking for in the way of suits ... what occasions you had in mind for wearing them at ... what impression you were trying to create ... what colours and materials and styles and textures suited you best ... how much money you wanted to spend on your suit ... and so on.

Do you think, Mr MD, that you might be more inclined to spend time with my second suit salesman than the noisy first one? Might you even want to try on a couple of suits? And possibly do some business?

Of course, you're not in the suit business. You're in the printing business. You just happen to be using words to sell your services.

Now I know a wordsmith who would suit you better. And by the way, pull in some business. Unless you'd rather carry on shouting.

Yours sincerely

MEL LEWIS

I never heard from Mr MD. I suspect it may have been the last sentence. It did rather put the boot in, don't you think?

I had been side-tracked by a current vogue in advertising, which is to sign off with a pun or a quip. For example, Peugeot ran an ad entitled, 'THE LAUNCH OF A FLAG-SHIP'. (Subtitled, 'FOR ALL YOU CAPTAINS OF INDUSTRY'.) They signed off, 'All of which should ensure you choose a Peugeot 505 V6. And avoid ending up in the same boat as everyone else.'

Trying to be clever, in business, you can end up looking wet.

The following letter *did* result in business. Note how much more measured the copy is. I still criticize, but I touch the nerve with a badger hair brush, not a toothpick. As well as the letter, I enclosed my self-publicity broadsheet, ('PROFESSIONAL PUBLICITY: AT A PRICE YOU CAN AFFORD'; see page 54).

Dear ... (managing director)

As a regular user of ... (his firm), largely on behalf of ..., my client, I was delighted to receive your newsletter recently;

It's an excellent idea and one with obvious benefits for your type of business.

I am writing to you now because it would be a pity if you did not take proper advantage of *all* the possibilities running such a publication opens up to you.

It is essential that such a newsletter coming from an organization such as yours should be as professional looking as possible. This is an area in which I have a good deal of experience, as you can see from the enclosed material.

As well as helping you in that respect, there is something else worth mentioning.

There is a service that you could offer which would

ensure that your newsletter becomes essential reading.

If these ideas interest you, let me know and we can talk some more.

Yours sincerely

MEL LEWIS

This is a low-key letter. But I planted something in the last paragraph that really raises the temperature. I promised a benefit that I did not spell out. Prospects may or may not be interested in what you have to offer. But they are certainly curious about their own businesses and how they can be improved.

The dangled promise earned me an interview, and I sold my way into employment.

A word of warning: never promise something you can't deliver!

Hit them with your USP
One of the catchwords of advertising, promotion and marketing, today, is 'positioning'. The only thing new about this concept is the word 'positioning'.

For years, there has been an equally poignant piece of jargon available: USP—unique selling proposition. The USP is what your product (or service) has that the competition doesn't have.

Sometimes, the USP is obvious. Coke, or Coca-Cola, has been effectively marketed as 'The Real Thing'. As the *original* cola, it has spawned scores of imitators. Here is a readily understood sales point.

'Coca-Cola is.' The follow-up campaign was one of those teasing, tantalizing—or intensely irritating, depending on how you view it—advertising ploys that invites you to complete a statement, having established in an earlier

75

campaign what the closing phrase should be. Whichever way you slice it, a USP is a potent element in selling technique.

A while ago, I was able to witness at first hand the effect of a USP on a client, the power of its simple message. On account of my position as antiques fairs correspondent for the UK's leading dealer and collector magazine (*Antique Dealer & Collector's Guide*, IPC Magazines), I was asked to research a possible new rendezvous for an antiques fairs organizer. It was a large showground in the Midlands, and I arranged to travel to the place to investigate it.

Suddenly, presumably for reasons of costs, my client decided he would somehow like me to do my job without actually going to the Midlands. How was I to persuade him that this was an inane proposition, and that there was no alternative but to go and see the place in person?

I decided to write to the client, telling him an apocryphal story, drawn from advertising copywriting lore.

> Dear . . .
>
> Let me tell you a little story. It's about a man who was to become a famous advertising copywriter.
>
> He was landed with the task of promoting a brand of lemonade. There was nothing special about this lemonade. In fact, it was no better, no worse, than a score of other fizzy drinks on the market. But our ad-man believed in research, in telling a story about his products . . . engaging the punter, grabbing interest.
>
> So he paid a visit to the bottling plant. There, he asked the foreman: 'What's this amazing machine? Why is it steaming? What's it doing?' Back came the reply: 'Oh, that's nothing special. It's a machine for steam cleaning the returned bottles. Everybody uses them.'
>
> Then the advertising man knew he had his story.
>
> He quickly discovered that it was true, all the other firms did steam clean their bottles. But no one

thought to write about it, to tell their customers what care was taken with those empties.

Our 'winner' prepared an ad that told it all: X brand bottles were 'thoroughly, hygienically steam cleaned'. It became one of the most successful, longest-running campaigns of all time. And it transformed the fortunes of the lemonade company.

And all because that advertising copywriter took the trouble to look.

That's why I need to go to. . . .

The letter did the trick. My client saw the light, I took the train north, wrote my report, then waited to get paid. And waited. And waited some more. When we were practically walking up the aisle of the magistrates court together, he did, finally, put his hand in his pocket.

Why was this?

Imagine a situation where a painter and decorator is suddenly told by a customer to do the work without using any paint. The painter wastes no time in walking away from that impossible job. I had *oversold* my client. Some jobs simply aren't worth having. I should have packed my 'brushes' and left sooner.

Mail-order techniques it will pay you to learn
If you are a retailer, there's no need for you to suffer in slack times. You can take a leaf out of the book of the big mail-order companies. They have tough times, too, but they ride them out better, because they don't wait for customers to come to them. They go to their customers through the post, and so can you—for nominal cost.

You should already have a list of customers. If not, start one today. All you need is a nice, thick 'Visitors' Book' whenever new clients—or even a 'looker'—walks in, ask for their names and addresses. Or put your book where it can be seen and easily written in, with a prominent notice asking for details.

Say *why* you want that information—because, from time to time, you announce special offers, new lines, and so on. Use the same argument when you ask for customers' names and addresses to write on their receipt—keeping a copy, of course! Tempt people with a price save or a novelty and they'll co-operate.

You can do lots of things with your mailing list. Herbie Frogg, clothiers in London's West End, mail their customers prior to a sale to invite them in early as a 'valued customer' bonus. L'Uomo Elegante, men's and women's fashion importers, run an ad in the London evening paper offering '10% off the reduced prices if you bring this ad'. Why not combine these ideas and slap even more cream on the cake? Invite customers to a sale goods *preview* with an extra cash-off sweetener.

The truth is, almost anything that is sold lends itself to this technique: books, DIY materials, typewriters, sports equipment, food. There's a grocery store in the USA that sends out a letter announcing reductions on all kinds of food, usually luxury items like smoked salmon, tinned lobster soup, or *home-made* pâté. The home-made pâté is always a draw. You can't get it at faceless supermarkets.

How about your letter? 'I'm not much good at letter writing', is a common cry. Good news—you don't have to be. You're in business and you're trying to pull in customers. You're not trying to win the Booker Prize for Literature. You just have to make an offer. Use simple language.

'*It's not what you say, it's the way you say it.*' No, the song is WRONG, when it comes to 'sell copy'. If you have an *intriguing offer*, a *strong message*, copy full of *intriguing good ideas*, you will communicate and motivate your reader regardless of your prose.

Tell the whole story, and see that your letter *looks* good. Any local printing shop will do you an inexpensive job. They'll type it out professionally and run off as many copies as you want. One important tip: don't start your letter 'Dear Sir or Madam', even though it's a circular letter. You want it to sound personal, so start, 'Dear Customer'.

Best news of all, you can start making use of the mail for profit for practically nothing. As a first time user of direct mail, the Post Office will give you up to 1000 free 'shots'— you pay no post! Phone your Head or District Postmaster (in London) and ask for a visit from the Postal Services Representative. With such a bargain bonus, make a resolution today: no more griping about slack business. Start using the post to 'bring 'em in'.

Some of the most important letters you write are reminders . . .

A successful collection technique must be the single, most effective way to improve the profitability of your business. Better cashflow will enable you to avoid loans and punitive interest rates . . . pay cash for goods and services and claim a discount . . . pay your own debts quickly, so enhancing your own credit standing.

However, your aim is not to get good at chasing money, but to become expert at *avoiding* trouble. The trick is to work backwards from the worst possible outcome: a frustrating and time-consuming court case.

In order to win in court you need to show, beyond a shadow of a doubt, that there was an agreement to do business, and a binding contract for payment, according to agreed terms. Many people do good business without pieces of paper 'on a handshake'. But if you try it, every so often you will lose some fingers. It always pays to 'get it in writing'.

Whenever you meet a client, send a follow-up letter outlining, in everyday language, what was said and agreed. If the deals, specifications, terms, conditions are changed, confirm that, too, in a further short letter—sent, for preference, by recorded delivery.

Don't call your demands 'invoices', call them 'bills'.

Better still is 'bill to pay', leaving no doubt about what action is required. Be sure to state to whom the cheque should be made out and where it is to be sent. Confusion is an excuse for delay, and unresolved queries are a key factor in slow and no payment.

Always state your terms. Precisely. Not 'net monthly', which could mean payment is due a month after the goods have arrived, a month after the invoice date, a month after the despatch of the goods, or a month after the end of the month in which the goods were invoiced or sent. You know when you want to be paid, so say it in plain English. If you mean a month after 1 June 1987, write 'pay on or before 1 July 1987'.

Membership for a trade protection organization, such as British Mercantile Credit, Station Road, Sidcup, Kent, will also strengthen your image and make you a less tempting target for tardy payers. A trader will fear that poor payment record could become common knowledge among business peers.

The Credit Protection Association, 350 King Street, London W6 0RX, issues special stickers, distinguished by a beady eye design, to fix to bills, envelopes and so on. The 'you are being watched' message can help show you mean business.

How to get a better letterhead

Your letterhead represents you—quite literally—in many places where you may never set foot. In the absence of your person, a piece of paper is all people have to go by. Does your business 'representative' serve you well?

Most are neat, clean and presentable enough, but many only do *half* a job of work. Looking through some old-fashioned American letterheads in *The Business Letter in Modern Form*, by William H. Butterfield, I am struck by the richness of the printing ... the probity that appears to glow from these engraved masterpieces that look, by no accident, like banknotes or share certificates. . . . But most of all, by the *appropriateness* of the illustration.

If a firm is in the belting business there are belts stacked on a floating 'plinth' in the design. A plumbing firm has a tap in its masthead. A brewery shows a beer bottle decanting its 'amber nectar' into a glass. There is no way anyone could mistake the line of trade of these firms.

A viable alternative, one adopted by De Moulin Bros & Co, Manufacturers of Uniforms and Equipment, is to show an illustration of their splendid factory in dramatic perspective. This is prestige advertising. The drawing telegraphs the message: we must be good, look how big and smart our premises are.

What passes for the then modern improvement in *The Business letter*, 1941 version, are mostly dull in comparison. Turn now to your own letter file and see how *eye-catching*, *memorable* or *apt* the letterheads are of people you've been doing business with.

Then turn to your own letterhead. Is that doing the best possible job for your business?

Inspired by the 'Letterhead Rating Chart' in the above book here are some Lewis tips to help you improve your 'letterhead quotient'.

1. If you don't show what you do in a picture, (computer screen for a hi-tech firm, for example), at least spell out what you do with *words*.
2. Show where you are—if that is an instantly recognizable location. This may be good news, if people associate that with a particular type of trade.

   Thus a picture of Fleet Street showing St Paul's from Ludgate Circus *used* to be perfect for a newspaper company logo. Now they've moved out to the Isle of Dogs, it's difficult to know what would be appropriate. . . .
3. If you cannot easily show what you do in a picture, you can at least show how stylish you are. Smith Bundy & Partners' water colour of their splendid Regency terrace

Smith Bundy & Partners Ltd.

ADVERTISING AND MARKETING

Figure 4.3 There are many ways to lift a letterhead out of the 'print only' rut. Smith Bundy & Partners, specialists in advertising and marketing, feature a superb watercolour sketch of their splendid South London Regency offices.

house in Kennington, South London, relays *class*. (See Figure 4.3)

4. Don't be lured by the formula:

expensive paper and printing = successful company.

Your clients and competitors will know you have money to burn (on the wrong things). Or they will conclude that you are putting up a front, but are really on your uppers. To add to which, your secretaries will hate you for having to reel all that knobbly, hand-laid paper through their machines.

5. If you must use embossed lettering, at least stick a colour on the embossment. I occasionally have had to take letters to the window for the sun to throw a

shadow across the logo so I can read the name of the company.

6. Focus on figures. More than once I have accidentally telephoned someone's Fax number. The ears ring painfully for hours after the experience. Now that many firms have Fax, electronic mail, telex, VAT and registration numbers—as well as telephone numbers and numbers of lines, get your designer to handle the layout of these figures with particular care.

7. If your letterhead really is your *doppelganger* through the door of your business associates, consider putting your face on it. I have for years (see Figure 4.4). And I'm not the only one. Prospective Parliamentary Candidate for Hackney North and Stoke Newington, Diane Abbott did, too. Now she's an MP. And so does my former writing colleague Aminatta Forna, with a little prompting from this writer.

You can't get more personal than your portrait. Yes, you will upset some people who think it's flash. But very few, and none you would want to do business with. 'Face paper', as I call mine, when I want my secretary to use that, as opposed to the blander 'Lewis Associates' stuff, achieves a number of very important goals which more than make up for any disadvantage.

Quite literally, and at a stroke, you have an extremely high profile in the in-tray. How often have you phoned to follow up a letter, only to discover that no one has seen it, no one knows who you are, and they don't much care, either? Well let me tell you, I don't suffer from that.

When I phone up I say, 'The name's Mel Lewis, I wrote to your boss on . . .' and I get the same blank reception. But then I say, 'You must have seen the letter. There's a picture of me looking like Rasputin in the top left-hand corner . . .' They *always* remember this, if they've seen the letter at all.

They also laugh, which is an added bonus, because secretaries are 'gate-keepers', protecting their bosses from

Mel Lewis
Editor-in-Chief
Editor's Choice Features Service

Lewis Associates
2 Dagmar Passage
London N1 2DN
01-359 5749

Contributor to:

The Daily Mail
Cosmopolitan
Harpers & Queen
Honey
The Magazine
City Limits
Girl About Town
Ms London
Chic
Root
The African Guardian
African Concord

Financial and Legal
Correspondent,
Parents magazine

Former Consumer
Correspondent
Femail, Daily Mail

Columnist,
Antique Dealer &
Collector's Guide,
IPC

Antiques columnist
Market Trader

And contributor to
the National Press,
including:
The Times
The Sunday Times
Colour Magazine,
    Daily Telegraph
Guardian
Daily Express
Evening Standard
Look Now
She
Men Only
Family Circle
Pix (Australia)

Mel Lewis is the
author of:
*How to Make
Money from
Antiques*
(Blandford)
*Collecting for Fun
and Profit*
(Proteus)
*How to Collect
Money that is
Owed to You*
(McGraw-Hill)

Editor's Choice Features Service
is a Division of Lewis Associates
VAT registration no. 299 3954 84

time-wasters and others. Yet that simple pictorial device has broken down an important barrier. Finding the letter, flagged by my face, and tracing its progress then becomes an easy matter.

Now do you see why I choose to stare at people off the printed page?

Figure 4.4   This high profile way of illustrating a letterhead meets with some resistance among the faint-hearted British—especially when you look like me, perhaps! The point is though that it separates you from the pack and makes your correspondence instantly more memorable. And if you happen to be as lovely as my former writing associate Aminatta Forna no one seems to complain. The bottom line is that the more personal and approachable you are, the more business you do—regardless of how you look.

5. How to spot (and then write) a good advertisement

These simple tips will help you detect good advertising even before you may understand *why* it is good.

1. The company keeps repeating the same ad. (Advertising is expensive; most businesses don't throw money away on a continuing basis.)
2. It appears in roughly the same form in a variety of media. (It has already shown its 'pulling power' and is being tested elsewhere.)
3. It doesn't change much over a period of time.
4. It is imitated.
5. It is 'wordy', has few pictures.
6. It *doesn't* win advertising industry awards.
7. It seems to work hard for its money.
8. It is full of the word 'you'.

Advertising has just two aims. To sell more product or—which comes to the same thing in the long run—track down more prospects.

This section is not a treatise on advertising. But if you seriously want to track down more prospects, read it carefully. The tips, or rather strategies, it contains are tried and proven. Over the years, they've helped advertisers find millions of prospects. They'll help you, too.

Tip 1 The headline can make or break your advertisement
Let that sink well in. Because if you fail to attract the attention of the kind of people you want to read your advertisement, the rest of your work is wasted. The 'body copy' can be a poem of sales technique. But if it isn't read, it's dead—

and so are your chances of getting the most out of your advertisement. (See Figures 5.1 and 5.2)

Your headline must do two things: define your market and promise benefits. Take this famous headline: 'How I Retired On A Guaranteed Income For Life'. It identifies its target—people who want to retire—and promises a real hot benefit—guaranteed income for life. All that in just nine words.

Here's a variation on the same theme: 'You Don't Have To Be Rich To Retire On A Guaranteed Income for Life'. Notice something about the second variation? It's got 14 words. Too long? No. There's no such thing as a headline that's too long—only a headline that wins for you or loses. A good headline can work wonders wherever you use it— on your advertising to flag your sales letters, on brochures, and so on:

> On the average, five times as many people read the headlines as read the body copy. It follows that unless your headline sells your product, you have wasted 90 per cent of your money—*David Ogilvy, head of Ogilvy & Mather, one of the world's biggest advertising agencies.*

But how do you know what is a good headline? Which is the best headline? One thing is sure: tip-top headlines do not, normally, fall out of the back of the typewriter. They require work, sweat, spit and polish. Even the front-page title on the house journal of The Porchester Group took some getting to—as you can see from the actual work sheet from which the chosen heading was taken (see Figure 5.3).

This doesn't necessarily mean going to the library or the cuttings file. It does mean jotting down everything that comes into your head that relates to the subject in hand.

Suppose you are marketing business diaries, your quick list might feature the following:

While Saatchi & Saatchi are the most celebrated advertising agency in the country, Miller & Kendall are merely the most recent.

While Saatchi & Saatchi are a global empire, we are no more than a small independent state.

And while Saatchi & Saatchi have taken over numerous other agencies, we have just taken over new offices.

But one of the eternal joys of advertising is that, where it appears, the great and the small suddenly become the same size.

This double page spread has exactly the same dimensions for Miller & Kendall as it would have for Saatchi & Saatchi.

No agency can make a 48 sheet poster any larger, or make a 30 second TV spot any longer.

All they can do is produce advertising which makes those spaces work harder.

If advertising has impact, originality and relevance, it can reach out to touch the consumer's perceptions and purse-strings. Regardless of the agency or client behind it.

If it doesn't, being placed by a monster agency or paid for by a mega-corporation won't prevent it shrinking into nothingness.

DON'TS & DO'S

At Miller & Kendall, we don't have floors full of account managers, media people, planners, secretaries and administrators.

We don't pretend to have the capacity (or the desire) to take over our clients' marketing or PR or pack design.

We do, however, have a wealth of experience gained in both extremely large and extremely small agencies, working on accounts varying from the most celebrated household names to brand leaders in highly specialised and technical markets.

We do have a well-established working relationship with the London Media Company, one of the top media independents, giving us enviable planning expertise and buying power.

We do have the same access to the best research companies, production companies, photographers, type houses and other essential services as anyone else.

And we do have some unshakeable beliefs.

That advertising which seeks to attract attention through a freshness of thought or execution is more

Figure 5.1 Selling yourself or your business takes a special kind of skill. When in doubt, fill your space with *facts*. Such as who your clients are ... sales figures ... how special or cheap your services are. You'll never go wrong selling on benefits. New advertising

MILLER & KENDALL ARE NOW AS BIG AS SAATCHI & SAATCHI.

involving than advertising which does not.

That advertising which deals with intelligent propositions will be more persuasive than advertising which deals in vacuous rhetoric or empty imagery.

That advertising which treats its audience with respect and understanding will win more friends than advertising which condescends or hectors or dissembles.

And that (despite the evidence of most advertising to the contrary) there are many clients who share these beliefs.

Of course, there will always be accounts that want their advertising to be co-ordinated from Milwaukee to

Macao. Or need thirty dealer support ads a day. Or like the reassurance of platoons of executives pouring their coffee and laughing at their jokes.

Miller & Kendall will be of absolutely no interest to such clients.

But if you want your advertising to get you noticed and remembered, call managing director Lance Miller or creative director Paul Kendall on 01-437 8477 to arrange to see more of our work.

After all, you've just seen us do it for ourselves. Why shouldn't we do it for you?

M I L L E R ✚ K E N D A L L

MILLER & KENDALL ADVERTISING LIMITED, 63-65 RIDING HOUSE STREET, LONDON W1P 1PP. TELEPHONE: 01-437 8477.

agency Miller & Kendall went one better. They incorporated their facts into a convincing *argument* in this eye-catching *Campaign* advertisement.

Is there room for another quality daily?

TONY ALLEN-MILLS
New York Correspondent, **Daily Telegraph 1984-86**

NICHOLAS ASHFORD
Diplomatic Correspondent, **The Times 1985-86**

PATRICK BARCLAY
Football Correspondent, **Today 1985-86**

ANTHONY BEVINS
Political Correspondent, **The Times 1981-86**

LORNA BOURKE
Personal Finance Editor, **The Times 1981-86**

DAVID BREWERTON
Chief Investment Writer, **Daily Telegraph 1978-86**

ANDREW BROWN
Chief Reporter, **Spectator 1984-86**

COLIN BROWN
Political Reporter, **The Guardian 1979-86**

MAGGIE BROWN
The Guardian 1980-86

JOHN BULLOCH
Middle East Correspondent, **Daily Telegraph 1969-86**

CHARLES BURGESS
Deputy Sports Editor, **The Guardian 1985-86**

ALEXANDER CHANCELLOR
Deputy Editor, **Sunday Telegraph 1986**

RUPERT CORNWELL
Chief Bonn Correspondent, **Financial Times 1984-86**

MICHAEL CROZIER
Editor, Special Projects, **The Times 1985-86**

JO DAVIS
Energy Editor, **The Economist 1985-86**

SEBASTIAN FAULKS
Feature Writer, **Sunday Telegraph 1983-86**

JONATHAN FENBY
Paris/Bonn Correspondent, **The Economist 1982-86**

JAMES FENTON
Chief Book Reviewer, **The Times 1983-86**

Figure 5.2   When *The Independent* was launched it was a well-known trade secret that many *Times* writers were being attracted away from 'Fortress Wapping' to a work situation that was not also a 'hard-hat' area—the print unions were still smarting at their summary dismissal and were creating mayhem outside Rupert

48 of Britain's top journalists think so.

Nicholas Garland
Political Cartoonist, **Daily Telegraph 1966-86**

Terry Garrett
Company News Editor, **Financial Times 1979-86**

Oliver Gillie
Medical Correspondent, **Sunday Times 1972-86**

Stephen Glover
Foreign Feature Writer, **Daily Telegraph 1981-85**

Ian Griffiths
City Reporter, **Daily Mail 1986**

Sarah Helm
Home Affairs & Political Reporter, **Sunday Times 1986**

David Hewson
Arts Correspondent, **The Times 1983-86**

Gabriel Hilton
Assistant Foreign Editor, **Sunday Times 1985-86**

Sarah Hogg
Economics Editor, **The Times 1984-86**

Ken Jones
Chief Sportswriter, **Sunday Mirror 1972-86**

Tom Kyte
Questor Column Writer, **Daily Telegraph 1977-86**

Nigel Lloyd
Managing Editor, **Observer 1979-86**

Donald Macintyre
Labour Editor, **The Times 1985-86**

Fiona Maddocks
Assistant Commissioning Editor, **Channel 4 1985-86**

Christopher McKane
Chief Home Sub-Editor, **The Times 1982-86**

Jane McLoughlin
Industrial Relations Correspondent, **The Guardian 1985-86**

John Moore
City Correspondent, **Financial Times 1982-86**

Geoffrey Nicholson
Sports Writer, **The Observer 1978-86**

Michael Prest
Financial Correspondent, **The Times 1982-86**

Robert Rice
Editor, **New Law Journal 1981-86**

Audrey Slaughter
Editor, **Working Woman 1984-86**

Edward Steen
Senior Foreign Feature Writer, **Sunday Telegraph 1980-86**

Thomas Sutcliffe
Editor, Kaleidoscope, **BBC Radio 4 1985-86**

Matthew Symonds
Chief Economics Leader Writer, **Daily Telegraph 1981-85**

Nicholas Timmins
Social Services Correspondent, **The Times 1983-86**

John Torode
Leader Writer, **The Guardian 1976-86**

Andrew Whitam Smith
City Editor, **Daily Telegraph 1977-85**

Peter Wilby
Education Correspondent, **Sunday Times 1977-86**

Neil Wilson
Sports Writer, **Daily Mail 1980-86**

Peter Wilson Smith
Banking Correspondent, **Daily Telegraph 1985-86**

WHAT HAS MADE THESE journalists, and over 100 more, leave their secure, well-paid jobs to write for a newspaper that doesn't even exist yet? The answer will appear on Tuesday the seventh of October 1986.

THE INDEPENDENT

CONTACT ADRIAN O'NEIL, THE INDEPENDENT, NEWSPAPER PUBLISHING PLC, 40 CITY ROAD, LONDON EC1Y 2DB, TELEPHONE 01-253 1222

Murdoch's new printing plant on the Isle of Dogs. This advertisement, which appeared in *Campaign*, uses a very bullish format and demonstrates forcibly the power of personal endorsement allied to a sales message.

TYRRELL

TEAMWORK
TURBOCHARGED PORCHESTER
POWER
PORCHESTER POWER!
FAZTES GROUP INTHE WEST
CAR
RACING COLOURS
COLOUR SUPPLEMENT
FLAG UP ... DOWN
AHEAD OF THE PACK
BRITISH
DESI N
POWER PACKED
PORCHESTER S LATEST PACKAGE
BRITISH GRAND PRIX

SILVERSTONE
RACIN COLOURS
FLAG BEARING
PROMOSING START
FLYING START
SUMMER MADNESS
SEASON'S
TRACK
FINS UP, SECONDS AWAY
POWER PACKED PORCHESTER!
SECRET WEAPON
BALIS
T E PORCHESTER EFFECT
ON THE RIGHT TRACK
FAST LANE
SPONSORSHIP
POWER BEHIND THE TYRRELL
H W PORCHESTER BOOSTED A TURBO
SUPERPOWER
PORCHESTER SUPERPOWER!
POWER AND THE GLORY
WE HAVE LIFT OFF!
ROUND

EYE ONTHE BALL
DRIVE
ROUND ROBIN
CIRCUIT
PACKAGE TOUR
GRAND PRIX PORCHESTER
PORCHESTER THE BIG ONE
ANOTHER PORCHESTER HIGH PERFORMER!
A LIFE INTHE DAY OF THE PORCHESTER GRO P
CARRYING THE FLAG
PORCHESTER
THE DAY PORCHESTER WENT TO THE RACES
A DAY AT THE RACES
PORCHESTER'S DAY AT THE RACES
COVER STORY
FASTEST COVER INTHE WEST
HOW PORCHETSER CARRIED THEFLAG
AT T EBRITIWH GRANDPRIX
GRAND PRIX PORCHESTER!

ABSOLUTE
FULL STORY
CENTRE PAGES

SEE CENTRESPREAD STORY

Porchester live!
Journal of The Porchester Group
Volume 1 No. 3

GRAND PRIX PORCHESTER!

Full Story
Centre Pages

- Year planner.
- Plenty of room to write appointments.
- Each hour divided up into quarter-hour sections.
- Leather bound.
- Clip fastening works every time, no fumbling.
- Extra large diameter ring binding.
- Compatible with other desk diary systems.
- Useful pockets for business cards, credit cards, etc.
- Personalizing service: Gold blocked initials.

You get the picture. Assuming you are searching for a headline, you might then home in on the line: 'Each hour divided up into quarter-hour sections'. Your new list reads:

- Time saving.
- Punctual.
- Manage your time.
- Use every moment of your day.
- Time is money.
- Busy.

This list might yield the headline:

> The only business diary that helps you manage
> every moment of your busy day

There's news value, USP—Unique Selling Proposition, this is the *only* diary that does this—clearly-targeted user benefits, and so on. All the rest of the features you've written down, which don't make it to your headline, are still

---

Figure 5.3 The way to a successful and eye-catching heading is often down rivers of sweat and blood. The title on the cover of The Porchester Group's journal, *Porchester Live!*, which I write and produce, did not, as you can see, 'fall out of the back of the typewriter', however 'obvious' and right it may now seem. Even the simple title of this book took three weeks' (thankfully intermittent) head-banging to produce.

usable: these will be woven into your 'body' copy, sales letter, brochure copy, etc. Work on improving your headlines, and they'll always work for you.

So your headline has attracted the attention of genuine prospects. What next?

Tip 2   *Don't let your reader down*
You'd be surprised how many advertisements have body copy which bears little or no relationship to the headline.

You've promised a benefit in the headline. Continue to promise benefits—the more the merrier. Sell benefits *not* your product. Benefits are what the product can do for your prospect—happy retirement ... peace of mind ... money for his children's education ... and scores more.

Do you know every benefit your product offers? If not, now's the time to find out what they are and list them. That way you'll never miss a trick when preparing your body copy.

Tip 3   *Keep yourself in the background*
If you really need to tell your prospects how big your firm is, how many millions there are behind it, do it quietly and in passing. Your prospects are interested in themselves ... what you can do for them.

Here's a tip every real professional copywriter bears in mind: the more 'we' and 'I' in an advertisement, the less chance it has of succeeding; the more 'you' in your advertisement, the more chance of success it has.

Talk to your prospects about what they will gain by acting on your advertisement. By the way, if there's something your prospects will lose by not acting, get that in, too. People hate losing.

Tip 4   *Keep humour out of your advertisement*
'Make 'em laugh' is a wonderful slogan for stand-up comics. But being funny has no place in your advertisement. Money is a serious matter to your prospects.

Especially *their* money. Be funny about it and you'll never be treated seriously—worse, you will even be looked on suspiciously.

Wouldn't you shy away from people asking you to trust them with your money, while making jokes about it?

By the way, you'll get plenty of people who'll tell you you should be light-hearted. Ignore them. They're not even amateurs. They are know-nothings.

Tip 5 *Call for action—now*

This is hard to believe, but I've read scores of really good advertisements which fell down at the end. They failed to ask decisively for action—now. Tell your prospects exactly what you want them to do. Don't just stick a coupon at the end of your advertisement—tell your readers to fill it in.

Tell them twice, three times, 10 times if necessary. And tell them to do it today, this very moment. If you want them to phone—give a name or an extension to ask for. (Incidentally, make sure that whoever answers the phone gets the name of the caller right. Nothing irritates a prospect more than being addressed by the wrong name.)

And while we're on the subject of getting names right— always tell your prospects to write their names and addresses in *block letters*. Plenty of advertisers overlook this. Result? Unreadable writing. And a prospect lost. So tell your readers to print clearly. At today's advertising rates, prospects are costly enough to come by. Every one you lose actually increases the rate still further.

Now here are some ways you can improve your coupon. If you are offering a brochure and you've spoken about the value of it in your body copy (as you should), mention it again on the coupon. If no salesperson will call, say so— not just in the advertisement but on the coupon. Remember, too, give your prospects as much room to write as possible. The coupon has a big part to play in the success of your advertisement. It can pay you to cut body copy in order to accommodate a bigger coupon.

Talking about cutting, remember to leave in your own name and address on the advertisement—*in the right position*. It will help you win even more prospects.

The name and address of your company should always appear at the end of the body copy and well clear of the coupon. The reason is obvious. You don't want your name and address cut out with the coupon.

Magazines especially have a 'secondary life'. They circulate after the original readers have finished with them. If the original reader has cut out your name and address, nobody else has a chance to answer your advertisement.

One last and important tip. Even if you yourself don't write your advertisements, at least learn what makes a good prospect-pulling advertisement. The basics have been given you in this section. By learning everything you can about *professional* advertising writing, you'll know if you're getting the real thing from your agency or your copywriter. If not, consult someone who can give you advertisements which bring in prospects.

Study successful direct mail

Look at advertising that includes a coupon, and the sales material sent to you through the post. Some of the biggest advertising agencies are wary of producing mail-order ads. The results are too easy to quantify! A mail-order ad either pulls and makes a profit. Or it flops for all to see. Direct-mail advertising has to work hard for its money—and so do the copywriters. Their hard work, their ads, are an open book to you the business writing enthusiast.

Appeal to the selfish streak in people

Never mind whether or not you like the idea that people are selfish, accept that it is 'the way of the world'. Read books like *Winning Through Intimidation* by Robert J.

Ringer, *The Selfish Gene* by Richard Dawkins, or Ayn Rand's, *The Virtue of Selfishness*. As Ringer points out:

> ... reality isn't the way you wish things to be, nor the way they appear to be but the way they actually are ... you either acknowledge reality and use it to your benefit or it will automatically work against you.

People part with hard-earned money for any or a combination of all of these reasons: To ... attract the opposite sex ... protect possessions ... experience pleasure ... earn and save money ... enjoy rude health ... be on a par with peers ... win the respect of those they respect ... win and sustain reputation ... avoid trouble and escape hardship ... be popular, win praise and avoid criticism ... fulfil themselves ... own beautiful objects ... be stylish ... save time and avoid effort ... take advantage of opportunities ... satisfy curiosity.

Relate any of these to an aspect of the goods or service you are retailing and you will have an identifiable and winsome benefit to build up in your copy.

If you want to interest people, talk about MONEY, FOOD, SEX, HEALTH, and anything that relates to those fundamentally appealing topics. Money suggests SUCCESS ... PRESTIGE ... FAME. FOOD could relate to FINE WINE ... ENTERTAINING. Put the two together and you arrive at GOOD FOOD ON A BUDGET.

SEX isn't just 'the act'; it's also LOVE ... RELATION-SHIPS ... MARRIAGE ... A HAPPY HOME ... CHILDREN. HEALTH can mean PHYSICAL or MENTAL HEALTH ... RECREATION, SPORT.

If you can harness your subject matter to any of these ideas and involve your readers personally, they will be 'all eyes'.

Talk to the person who matters most to your reader—him- or herself. Look at it another way, who do you put first in this world, business or otherwise? A single person might, with hand on heart, be able to say 'Mum'. But for most people, No. 1 comes first. It's natural. Just as, for a family man or woman, it would be normal to put wife or husband and children first. So 'you'—and 'yours'—are a pretty high priority.

Similarly in business, you will put first your own interests and those of your company. And you would expect those with whom you deal to do the same? You'd be right! They do. Then why not appeal to that sense of self at every turn? Not only should you emphasize the benefit for the other party in every business letter, but you should bring in those most riveting words, 'you' and 'yours', as early on as possible. They will guarantee you a spellbound audience. Here are some examples:

> *Your* orders for our goods . . .
> *You* have been paying . . .
> *Your* welcomed first order . . .
> *Your* outstanding balance . . .

How to handle a hairbrush . . . or any advertising assignment
Here is a mini example of the four main different ways of ordering material. The product (but it could just as easily be a service) happens to be a new type of hairbrush (fictional).

I have listed the various user-benefits which are to feature in a small trade paper ad. The list may be incomplete, but given the space and the object of this exercise, it is full enough. Here is the list:

Brush benefits
Broken/worn tufts can be replaced
Can be washed in washing machine
Bristles fold flat
Goes in pocket or handbag
Clip-on handle for long-hair brushing
Half the cost of comparable size bristle brush
Available in five colours

Buy two, get one free
Red, blue, yellow, green, beige
The price
The price
New kind of hairbrush to carry anywhere
Attractive enough for dressing table
Buy two (get three): one each for bedroom, bathroom, pocket/bag

That is a fairly typical benefits list. I have set them down as they came into my head, as I normally would.

Note 'The price' is written twice. That's because I want it to feature in the sub-heading under the main headline of the ad, and also in the body copy.

The sentence 'New kind of hairbrush to carry anywhere' is just a dummy: it reminds me that I need an attention-getting opening sentence which introduces the product.

As you will appreciate, the copy points could just as easily be sentences ... or paragraphs .... It is the *ordering* of the material that is under investigation here.

In what sequence will I present the various sales points in my advert?

Having chosen the sequence, I may write the sentences or part-sentences containing the benefits in any order I choose. (I might start writing about the washing machine, because that's the most outrageously original benefit, and it tickles me), and then 'stitch' them together according to the order I have chosen.

Here then is how I arrange these copy points/benefits.

Method one: the Spaghetti Western method

The 'spaghetti' method is useful (see Figure 5.4). But when you have quite a few points (as here), or you change your mind … it can start looking like Alice and the kitten with a ball of wool … You will probably have to retype the list anyway to make sense of it.

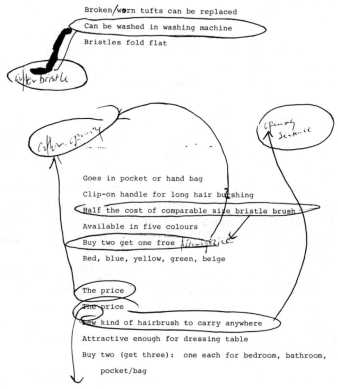

Broken/worn tufts can be replaced
Can be washed in washing machine
Bristles fold flat

Goes in pocket or hand bag
Clip-on handle for long hair brushing
Half the cost of comparable size bristle brush
Available in five colours
Buy two get one free
Red, blue, yellow, green, beige

The price
The price
New kind of hairbrush to carry anywhere
Attractive enough for dressing table
Buy two (get three): one each for bedroom, bathroom,
    pocket/bag

Figure 5.4

Method two: the laaaaaazzzzzeeee way

What normally happens is that you start off with good intentions, or are even inspired (see Figure 5.5). You put A,B,C, because you know the order you want. Then you have second thoughts. It still ends up looking like Spaghetti Junction.

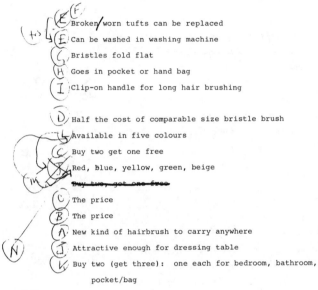

Broken/worn tufts can be replaced
Can be washed in washing machine
Bristles fold flat
Goes in pocket or hand bag
Clip-on handle for long hair brushing

Half the cost of comparable size bristle brush
Available in five colours
Buy two get one free
Red, blue, yellow, green, beige
~~Buy two, get one free~~

The price
The price
New kind of hairbrush to carry anywhere
Attractive enough for dressing table
Buy two (get three): one each for bedroom, bathroom,
pocket/bag

Figure 5.5

Method three: apple pie order

You simply put a letter against each point, in A–Z order, and then juggle the points in your head, till you come up with a 'final' running order (see Figure 5.6). The lists on the right show the various failed attempts, crossed out and the approved version.

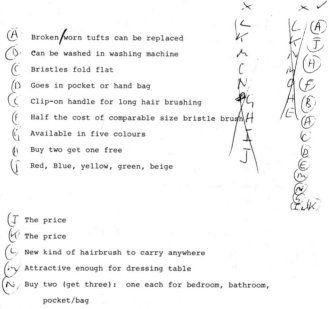

(A) Broken/worn tufts can be replaced
(B) Can be washed in washing machine
(C) Bristles fold flat
(D) Goes in pocket or hand bag
(E) Clip-on handle for long hair brushing
(F) Half the cost of comparable size bristle brush
(G) Available in five colours
(H) Buy two get one free
(I) Red, Blue, yellow, green, beige

(J) The price
(K) The price
(L) New kind of hairbrush to carry anywhere
(M) Attractive enough for dressing table
(N) Buy two (get three): one each for bedroom, bathroom, pocket/bag

Figure 5.6

Method four: cut the cackle, use paper and scissors!
All I did was type the points on a different piece of paper
each. I spread them on my desk (see Figure 5.7). Juggled
them about, then cut them out and pasted them down for
your benefit, to fit in this book.

But you could simply staple the pages together and work
from that. With one benefit per page, you can also use the
white space around to write in other subsidiary copy
points. Remember: time is precious. Not paper.

New kind of hairbrush to carry anywhere

The rice

Buy two get one free

Half the cost of comparable size bristle brush

Can be washed in washing machine

Broken/worn tufts can be replaced

Bristles fold flat

Goes in pocked or hand bag

Clip-on handle for long hair brushing

Attractive enough for dressing table

Buy two (get three): one each for bedroom,
bathroom, pocket/bag

Avaialable in five colours

Red , blue, yellow, green, beige

The price

Figure 5.7

6. *Writing reports and proposals*

There are many sorts of reports and proposals (the same creature, for my purposes here): technical ones, commenting on the latest processes for investigating banded bituminous coal; reports on the work performance of personnel; on the viability of business projects; and others, too numerous to mention.

I make no pretence at offering advice on each of them individually, only some pointers towards making *any* report more lively, more 'readable', and, *ergo*, more effective.

Remember this: reports suffer from the same malaise as most attempted deals: nothing results from them. If you are lucky enough to be in a position where your reports are paid for, regardless of the outcome, as I often am, good and well. Or they may be part of your larger employment, and fee is not in question, they just have to get written. *WRONG!* They should also get *READ*—if you want to produce something that is more than mere filing-cabinet fodder.

For this section, I am indebted to Hubert Bermont, author of *The Successful Consultant's Guide to Writing Proposals and Reports*. It is a model of clarity and presentation, as you might expect. I echo some of the points Mr Bermont makes, together with some of my own observations and a sample of a Bermont-inspired report and covering letter.

Remember what I said in the opening pages of this book: 'Learn by the mistakes of others, not your own'. The corollary is, 'It is better to imitate success than create mediocrity'. Once you know something is right and good, take it on board and stick it in your backpack.

Here, then, are 10 steps towards better, more readable, more effective reports:

1. Always include a covering letter (or a covering memo, if this is an 'internal' report). This is the equivalent of the handshake when you enter a business meeting. It re-establishes contact and also reminds your client/boss what the report is all about. And more, the letter should also *sell* the report, so the reader goes straight from the letter to the report.
2. State your credentials. Hubert Bermont's covering letter also features a 'partial list' of clients. If there is some way of re-establishing your credentials for writing the report, without being brassy, do so.
3. What style should you choose? Your own. Be yourself. The chances are that the reason you won this commission was at least in part due to your 'winning personality'. Why affect a different one to pursue the job?
4. How long should a report be? As long as you need to make your points. That could be a two-pager for a report on a revised milk round. Or 22 pages for building a new dairy-farming complex. The ambition should be to be concise, given the scale of the job in hand. People aren't as dumb as we may like to think. They know when something is being puffed up to make it look impressive, worth the fee, and so on. Don't insult their intelligence. And don't waste two lots of time: theirs and yours.
5. Shouldn't a report be impersonal? They certainly are, normally. Full of, 'It has been concluded that', instead of 'I believe', and 'It will be appreciated that', instead of the more familiar 'As you can see'.

   If you would normally put on a frock coat, top hat and tote a cane to address your bosses, by all means write like a stuffed shirt.

6. What should you call your report? In earlier days, I was asked to report on a new shopping complex. I called my story, REPORT ON ... PARADE. What a bore! I called a more recent, post-Bermont report

    AN EFFICIENT AND PROFITABLE XXXX
    (name of the company)
    PR, PROMOTION AND MARKETING PLAN

Which do you think sounds more businesslike, more intriguing—to the client?

7. Don't put miniature chef's hats on your drumsticks. You might be forgiven for dressing up a crown of lamb but a 10-page report does not need a frontispiece, table of contents and appendix.

8. Don't tart up your report. Your words will work. Or not. Resist the temptation to slap it in a gold-tooled leather binder. A simple folder or plastic envelope, to keep the fingerprints off, will do fine.

9. If appropriate, always finish with the 'bottom line'. Ah ... the bottom line! Your fee, of course. Assuming the clients are impressed by your message, they will also be dying to know the damage.

10. Don't give the game away. If your livelihood depends, at least in part, on winning work based on accepted reports, it is foolish to say too much. The clients can forgo your services and do the job themselves, or commission someone cheaper than you. So say what you will do, but never offer your clients a *blueprint* of how to do it.

Covering letter
    xxxx
    Managing Director
    xxxxxxxx
    London

    30th December 19——

Dear xxxx

Attached is the proposal you requested at our meeting a couple of weeks ago.

I am sure you will agree that it covers the points we discussed. Additionally, I have come up with a few more ideas to help solve some of your marketing and promotional problems.

Some ideas are plain commonsense, given your type of business; other solutions reflect your unique situation and require some innovation and even some daring.

All in all, the proposal represents a comprehensive plan to put xxxx firmly on top.

It goes without saying that I would be both pleased and proud to serve your company in the implementation of these plans—and you already know, from my other xxxx assignments, that I pursue my work with energy and determination.

Please let me know your reactions as soon as possible (by our next meeting on 7 January, if at all possible), so that I can plan my time accordingly.

With best wishes,

Yours sincerely

MEL LEWIS

AN EFFICIENT AND PROFITABLE XXXX PR, PROMOTION AND MARKETING PLAN

I. *Capturing a Larger Market Share Using a Direct Approach*

XXXX's potential market is readily defined and therefore easily reached and propositioned. Where targeting can be so precise, direct mail is the obvious and effective route to choose. The aim is to show up XXXX as the best available option by establishing all XXXX's USPs, and by introducing your greatest USP—[a new computerized system].

A letter campaign will enable you to expand existing business ... disillusion competitor's clients ... and penetrate new markets. All mailing material should invite principals to XXXX for a demonstration, or offer a visit from a XXXX executive, free and without obligation.

II. *Achieve a Higher Profile in the Market Place*

XXXX is not in the normal market position of having to establish a personality from among a host of competitors. You are in an Avis/Hertz situation, without the also-rans.

The following XXXX suggestions are intended to establish XXXX as the first choice company in your field.

1. Competitions.
2. Sports sponsorship.
3. Academic sponsorship.
4. XXXX seminars.
5. Extending the scope and readership of XXXX newsletter.
6. Other in-house publishing activities.
7. 'Covert operations', such as my suggested photographic feature.
8. Increased 'street' and logo awareness.

III. *Discover New Areas of Profitable Activity*

There are two main ideas which should be explored urgently. Firstly, P.D.'s idea of establishing a features Press release 'library'—and charging customers for this unique XXXX service, which neatly extends the effectiveness of historic campaigns.

And secondly, to offer companies a low-price 'starter kit', as an easy introduction to XXXX's full range of services.

IV. *Time and Place*

I propose to implement all of the above recommendations in a year to 18 months. My fee for this is a 12-months' understanding payable in one of two ways: a £3000 retainer for a year's services and £20 per hour, plus justifiable expenses. Or a 12-months' understanding with a £4000 retainer payable in two £2000 instalments, six-monthly in advance, and £20 per hour, plus expenses.

Mel Lewis
Lewis Associates

7. How to write power-packed Press releases

The Press release is one of the most powerful publicity tools available to you; and also one of the cheapest. A Press release is your own news story, written on your own headed paper, or specially printed paper bearing your own logo. It is the nearest you may ever get to writing for a paper or magazine. So why are the vast majority of Press releases—the commonly quoted figure is 90 per cent—binned virtually on sight? All sorts of reasons:

1. What's newsy to you falls flat with the editor.
2. Your release goes to the wrong person. In the best of all possible worlds, wrongly delivered mail gets passed to the right person. In the real world it is often binned, to save time; filed and forgotten; or correctly delivered, but too late.
3. It arrives too late.
4. The story is intrinsically good, but so badly presented that the editor loses heart and gives up reading before stumbling on the point of it all.

My experience with Press releases was gained on both sides of the fence: as an editor, sub-editor, writer and reporter and working on national newspapers and magazines—and as a Press consultant entrusted with getting messages across for big-paying clients. I can now appreciate what both parties want from Press releases— but times change, and what pleases one set of people may irritate others. Therefore, it makes very sound sense to actually visit the offices of editors who have responded positively to your releases.

On the pretext of hand delivering a release—in itself an endearing gesture, if you don't outstay your welcome—ask the editor or correspondents what they like to see in a Press release, how copy should be presented, special angles that could find favour, personal dislikes, and so on.

Benefits of a Press release

Remember you're in charge when you send out a Press release. You control the timing, the content, tone, and the 'to whom'—who gets the information. You can think first before putting pen to paper—a far cry from the cut and thrust of the live interview. You can argue your case more easily, for no one interrupts you; and from a practical viewpoint, you save the Press reporters time, flicking through their own half-digested notes: your document is neat and clear. And if the reporters want a different angle or elaboration, the writer of the release can be traced through the phone number you provide, at the foot of the story.

What Press releases can do for you:

- Announce new products, innovations.
- Announce company personnel promotions.
- Announce product promotions.
- Announce new advertising, sales campaigns.
- Announce a move.
- Preview a report.
- Give depth to a previous announcement.
- Refute or explain something.
- Circulate company comment or speech, in advance of an event.
- Offer newsworthy snippets about staff (if someone in accounts is also a prize-winning gardener, photo-

grapher, or sportsperson, that might rate a release and get the name of your business into print, by association).

Writing a Press release, the nuts and bolts

The intro

An 'intro' is the first paragraph or few paragraphs that lead the reader into the story. In newspapers the intro is often a larger type size than the rest of the story and sometimes a bold (heavier, blacker) print style as well. The main points of the story are contained in these opening sentences. The editor, or more likely the chief sub-editor or sub-editor plays the best cards in the opening words to draw you into the story and keep you reading. The more popular the paper (*The Sun, Daily Mirror*) the more licence the journalists have to 'flam up', or sensationalize their stories. The more sober broadsheet dailies (*The Times, The Guardian*) and Sunday papers (*Observer, The Sunday Telegraph*) tend to be more restrained.

The other point of getting the main elements of a story across in the first few words is that readers in a hurry can pick up the gist of the thing even if they don't read on. The tabloids are adept at stripping the clothes from the meat in the first few words; they need to be, because they have less room in their headlines to spell out what the story is about. For example, an item about cricketer Ian Botham slipping on the grass as he runs up to bowl might merit the headline, 'BOTHAM SLIPS UP IN BOWLING RUN UP' in *The Guardian*. *The Sun* might simply print 'OOPS!' in gigantic type, together with a picture that tells the whole story at a glance.

Your Press releases must similarly yield their message almost at a glance, by means of graphic words and telegraphic sentences. Not only because the journalists who read your release, and hopefully act on it, are jaundiced readers, they have so much of it to do for their own work, but also because experience tells them that most Press releases are badly written and not very newsy to boot. So it will pay you to put your best points up front, which enables the busy professional to make a quick decision and not waste valuable time.

Who, what, why, when, where and how

The Press release breaks one of the cardinal rules of good writing, that the story should follow on smoothly, inexorably, from the headline. This is one of the most important lessons business writers can learn from good advertising.

The thinking behind this rule is simple. The headline should attract and intrigue, but you should not keep your reader hanging about waiting for the promise of the title to be fulfilled. So an advertisement entitled 'BALD?' reads on 'Grow new hair in weeks with ...'.

Curiously, newspaper and magazine journalists are among the worst sinners in this area. The sub-editor, whose job it usually is to write a headline, will hit on an angle buried deep in the story, and paraphrase it in the heading. The readers wait and wait for the title to be explained, and it often isn't until they reach the foot of the text that the punchline appears.

At worst, and as frequently happens in amateurishly-run newspaper offices, the paragraph that furnished the headline idea is cut, so the readers *never* get the point of the headline! With monthly magazine journalists, working to a fairly relaxed deadline, there is no excuse for 'muff diving' for a title; the newspaper sub can at least plead lack of time.

It has been suggested that the readability of newspapers would be dramatically improved if the headlines and intro copy were written hand in glove. The great problem with newspapers, of course, is that the reporter writes the story, while the sub-editor tacks on the heading at a later stage. You, as a writer of Press releases are omnipotent, but still some break that golden rule. Why? Not because of lack of time, but because the reader, the journalist who receives your release, *is* hard pressed. So you tease with the heading, to attract attention, but revert to a formula in the intro, because in the end, the journalist will decide whether to read on and pursue your story (on the phone, or by sending out a reporter) on the strength of the hard facts presented, not your clever ways with words.

These facts are the 'WHO, WHAT, WHY, WHEN, WHERE AND HOW' of your story, though they are not necessarily presented in that order. Many Press release writers try to get all of these points into the first sentence, so guaranteeing an opening with all the visual attraction of an anaconda.

Instead, use two or three short sentences and break them up, if you like, into several paragraphs.

PORCHESTER SETS UP 'MONEY FOR BUSINESS' SHOP IN LONDON, WEST ONE

The Porchester Group, the UK life-broking giant, has established a highly successful commercial finance department at its Wimpole Street Branch in London's West End.

In operation barely a month, the department has already arranged £6 million of loans for businesses as diverse as farming, grocery retailing, industrial estate management and a motor franchise operation.

The department is run in association with Frederick Hill & Associates Limited, who have specialized in commercial finance for many years. Their fees are among the lowest in the market, and Porchester handles all the insurance side.

'This "shops within shops" concept is part of our plan for rapid expansion. The commercial department reinforces Porchester's position as an in-house brokerage able to offer a total financial service', says Porchester Director Terry Harvey.

This breaks down:

WHO:	The Porchester Group.
WHAT:	Has established a highly successful commercial finance department.
WHY:	(Fourth paragraph) So Porchester, an in-house brokerage can offer a total financial service under one roof, and pick up the insurance business that results.
WHEN:	(Second paragraph) A month ago, now on a firm footing.
WHERE:	Wimpole Street, London, W1 (I spelt out W1 as 'WEST ONE' in the title, simply to make a longer, more pleasing second line.
HOW:	Working with Frederick Hill & Associates, specialists in commercial finance.

How to make your copy 'leap off the page'

The Standard, one of London's evening newspapers, has a vitriolic, anonymous column entitled *Londoner's Diary*. 'I try to throw away Press releases unread but occasionally something leaps out at the eye', Londoner quipped. You will notice the verb—*try* to throw Press releases away unread: there is anguish involved. 'Will the releases that look as uninteresting as all the others in fact have the nugget of news that makes my name—or at least a "down page" story' is the question that plagues cynical journalists.

Of course Londoner is writing tongue in cheek; every release is at least scanned. But the diarist, you notice, is interested only when something 'leaps out at the eye'. That, then, is the aim of the Press release writer who would be read. Having your news *reported* is, understandably, something of a greater luxury; there is simply so much competition.

So how do you make copy leap out? One thing is sure: the event announcement, etc., does not need to be earth-shattering in importance, although you must kick off with your strongest angle. To do this you use journalistic tricks against the journalists, to urge them to read on. Look at these four releases from my files.

The first has a question as a heading: 'HAVE YOU ANY IDEA HOW THE PRIM LITTLE WORLD OF ANTIQUES IS CHANGING?' Even if the journalists don't give a dog end about the antiques world, they have to read on. The first sentence is another spur to action, involvement: 'Take a look at the ad with this letter.' In the world at large, and in the world of letters in which you are dallying, by and large people do as they are told. So the ad gets looked at.

The next release, about Grand Prix motor racing, flicks another human nerve end: 'TYRRELL ... THE ONE YOU *ALMOST* MISSED.' People hate to miss things: witness the success of headlines urging the public to 'ORDER NOW TO AVOID DISAPPOINTMENT' ... 'DON'T MISS THIS FABULOUS OFFER' ... 'STOCKS LIMITED, ORDER TODAY', and so on.

Even more tantalizing is the 'relief' offered: the event was only '*almost*' missed. There is a chance to get back in on the act, whatever that was. And the copy begins to explain: 'you missed a great photocall ...'.

The third release is about an antiques fair. This was indeed something of an earth-shattering event, at least in the 'prim little world of antiques':

BIGGEST ANTIQUES FAIR EVER HELD
ON BANK HOLIDAY MONDAY

I hope you spotted the journalistic licence. It certainly wasn't the biggest antiques fair ever held, though it promised to be the biggest *London* fair ever held. But it was true that this was the biggest Bank Holiday fair ever. But the way we broke the lines made it rather more tantalizing than perhaps it deserved. But as they say, better dead than not read....

Superlatives, even qualified ones, will always ensure

116

interest—that's why *The Guinness Book of Records* is such a success, year after year. So even a local 'first' is interesting to news reporters if it takes place in the area.

HACKNEY'S FIRST 'FESTIVAL OF FAIRS'
GREAT SALE OF BOOKS AND ANTIQUES

'Festival of Fairs' sounds like a major happening, and also one to raise cynical eyebrows: will it ever get off the ground? But a great sale of books and antiques sounds real enough and journalists are said to be frustrated authors, so any mention of books rates a second look.

Every story has an angle, if you look for it—or luck finds it the two partners in Vortex, an art gallery cum artists' materials shop cum bookshop cum café, in one of London's lesser known boroughs, Stoke Newington, were anxious to establish their unusual venue. I suggested an antiques fair, a small-scale indoor show in the under-used art gallery, as a way of attracting interest from the Press. Wasn't the combination of services of Vortex intriguing enough in itself? Possibly, but editors are always having to fill 'news pages', and an event is the stuff of news. An actual happening offers the paper a story, by way of an announcement, and also an opportunity to write up the event, *after* the event. So happenings are good news for you and also for editors.

As you might expect, antique dealers are not noted for their keenness to break new ground, and my theory that we could attract a more ambitious element from nearby Islington, a noted antique district, was ill-founded. Nor were the Press intrigued by the fact that one partner in Vortex was studying for a PhD in American literature and the other was a former London taxi driver. So why did we get substantial and very useful publicity in *Time Out* magazine?

Partly because the paper announces up-coming events

(even if they don't take place), but mostly because I'd included an eye-catching *photograph*. The partners were busily sorting books from boxes into their relevant shelf slots, when I stepped into the shop one day, camera in hand. I told them to stop all that organization and pull out as many books as possible, strew them all over the floor and squat in the middle.

The chaos was astonishing and so were the pictorial possibilities, the light and dark contrasts of pages and book jackets, spines against spreads, and so on. *Time Out* used the picture (and story) half postcard size: the equivalent advertising space would have cost hundreds of pounds to buy.

A good joke goes down well
Another time, I was part of a team organizing an antiques event with a difference. The Reproduction Interior and Design Show (subtitled 'Yesterdays Styles by Today's Craftsmen') was certain to be interesting to antiques and furniture trade papers, but what angle would the national papers go for?

I assumed that most journalists would know that the antiques shown at an antiques fair of any standing are vetted for age and authenticity. At the Repro show we would have no antiques, so I dreamt up the idea of a vetting committee who would vet all the exhibits 'to ensure that nothing genuine was allowed in', and used that in a headline on a Press release. *The Times* liked the joke and rewarded us with a generous mention, in their diary column, 'PHS'.

It's all about angles
Start as you mean to go on. If you want to write an eye-catching title, list some impactful words: extraordinary, astonishing, remarkable, unusual, intriguing, crazy, new, cheap, dead. Similarly, if you want to write a Press release

that grabs attention, think angles—and get those down on paper, too.

If you have just opened new business premises, that will be great news to you, but it may not raise an editor's eyebrow unless you can pitch the right angle. A Tory MP's wife opening a left-wing bookshop is an angle. When antiques entrepreneur Bennie Gray discovered that the reason for the flooding in the basement of a premises he was about to turn into an antiques market was a lost tributary of the River Tyburn, he wrote that into a series of Press releases announcing the opening of his Bond Street emporium. In fact, he resurrected the stream—just a gravel-lined trough of water, in reality—but the Press acreage he gained from his astute news sense (and good luck) was priceless.

Caroline Penman runs the prestigious Chelsea, Brighton and West London antiques fairs, and also used to organize Ardingly the South Eastern Showground, one of the major trade events in the antique dealer's calender. Dealers anxious to jump the queue to get first crack at the goodies inside were a constant menace. Many booked stalls they never occupied, merely to get in ahead of the rush.

But a trade fair is one of many similar events, and antiques don't capture column inches unless it's a story of faking on a grand scale, fabulous attic finds or a theft of a priceless relic. Publicity consultant Tony Gill, working for Caroline Penman, hired a helicopter to ferry in some well-known buyers over the heads of the mob baying at the gate. Of course there was a photographer waiting to snap these determined 'gate crashing' dealers as they landed. The result was rare after-the-event publicity for Ardingly and Caroline Penman.

How to flag Press releases
If you use specially printed Press release paper, perhaps with a running strap saying 'NEWS' or 'PRESS RELEASE', you won't need too much else. Some writers call them

'NEWS RELEASE', or 'PRESS NEWS', or 'NEWS STORY'.

If you send releases rarely, one of the most effective and direct methods to achieve the desired effect, getting your story into the paper, is to forget about Press releases altogether, and simply send a personal *letter* to the news/ picture editor by name.

Editors always respond instinctively, positively to good headings. So pick out the news angle and write that into a heading on your letter, inserting it between the 'Dear ...' and the first paragraph. The editors will thank you for saving them the effort of having to wade through prose to get to the news point.

Take a tip (or three) from the experts in response

Who are these experts? The direct mail and mail-order companies. They fly or flop from the success or otherwise of their clip-the-coupon advertisements and sales letters that pull in cheques in the post. Not all of their techniques relate to press releases, but some certainly do. Such as:

- Offering a free gift.
- Using 'you' copy.
- Make your promise a believable one.
- Offer a benefit that the audience wants.
- Talk to your readers in their own language.

When you offer something free to the Press, it had better be something truly tantalizing. One of the best attended Press receptions I ever went to had a diamond as a raffle prize. But if all you are offering is news, make the promise a believable one. Don't suggest to the editors that they'll have a scoop story if they send a reporter to a product launch or factory opening. Talk soberly about your event, and suggest, merely, that the editors might get a useful 'down page' photograph, as so and so the well-known disc jockey will be opening the show. But if your firm is in the dredging business and you plan to launch a new dredging device with a display of female mud wrestlers from Paris, don't be shy about making a song and dance of the picture potential on offer!

Talk to editors in the language they understand—and the best way to discover what that is, is to talk to reporters and actually ask them about their work and what they are looking for in Press releases.

Illustration lifts your Press release

Having any sort of picture or graphic illustration lifts your release high from the rut of run-of-the-mill Press handouts, which are just typed paper. I used a similar photographic symbol for a photocall release aimed at achieving a Press turnout for the first race in Britain, the British Grand Prix at Silverstone, of the Tyrrell Renault, backed by insurance brokers The Porchester Group. A silhouette of a camera went on the right, a line drawing of the car, an unusual aerial view, went on the left, at a jaunty angle. I reduced the car image from a plan using the reduction facility of a normal office photocopying machine, then simply stuck this impromptu 'artwork' on to the master copy of the Press release, ready for over-printing on to the company's headed stationery.

The day after the event I sent a follow-up release to all of the papers which had not been represented at Tyrrell's headquarters in Surrey. I told them who had made the pilgrimage: 'You missed a great photocall yesterday, at the Tyrrell racing organization, Ripley, Surrey.

'Who didn't? TV: Thames News (Sport), FOCA (Spanish); photographers: *Daily Express*, *Daily Mail*, Press Association, Auto Sport, Central Office of Information, *Surrey Advertiser*, *Borehamwood Post*, Zoom Photographic; reporters: *The Sun*, *The Daily Telegraph*, CBC, ABC, Editor's Choice Features Service [myself!]; radio: Capital, County Sound.'

The list was not meant as a boast, but to underline the importance of the occasion. No news reporter likes to miss a story or an angle—especially when a rival has latched on to it.

For the follow-up release I used a picture of the car—the same over-head view—only this time the car looked as if it was scorching a path, racing across and off the page. A stunning image, it was simply achieved (see Figure 7.1). I found one of my small son's toy cars with wheels roughly the width of my Tyrrell car illustration, ran them through some linocut ink (black) to make it look as if the 'mud tracks' were the Tyrrell's.

I made sure that on my master there was a piece of paper the size of a coin in exactly the same spot and the same size as the Porchester Group's logo. I ran the inked wheels across the page and over the paper disc. When the ink was dry, I lifted the disc. When the release was over-printed the gold blocked Porchester logo looked as if it had been stamped *over* the tyre tracks.

Another detail, but one with considerable visual impact, was the use of a familiar logo for the keyword in the title. 'Tyrrell ... the one you almost missed.' Instead of typing the word Tyrrell, I cut a logo from the car company's own headed paper (with permission) reducing it on the photocopier and used it in my headline.

The eye of the motor racing journalist, and that of the picture editor would be drawn to that typestyle, for they'd seen it many times before when Ken Tyrrell himself had sent out mailings on his own paper for his own cars. Images telegraph their messages and save valuable editorial time.

Of course, you don't have to use images. The first release we sent out on the Tyrrell car had no images, but was the most successful of all. It had news angles that were so strong we got the Press running. It was a *British* car (Tyrrell), with a *British* driver (Martin Brundle), in a *British* race (British Grand Prix at Silverstone), backed by a *British* sponsor (The Porchester Group). It's only when you don't have such strong story lines that you will need to

12 July 1985

THE PORCHESTER GROUP
Porchester House
91 Wimpole Street London W1M 7DA
Telephone 01-493 9090

Tyrrell ... THE ONE YOU ALMOST MISSED

You missed a great photocall. Yesterday. At the Tyrrell Racing Organisation, Ripley, Surrey.

Who didn't?

TV: Thames News (Sport); FOCA (Spanish)

Photographers: Daily Express, Daily Mail, Press Association, Autosport, Central Office of Information, Surrey Advertiser, Borehamwood Post, Zooom Photographic

Reporters: Sun, Daily Telegraph, CBC, ABC, Editor's Choice Features Service

Radio: Capital, County Sound

Why did all these journalists turn up?

To view the new Tyrrell Renault Turbo. Tyrrell's first turbo-powered Formula One racing car -- making its first ever appearance on British soil.

The car is sponsored by The Porchester Group, Britain's biggest insurance broker. And raced by British driver Martin Brundle, 26.

The Tyrrell you "almost" missed?

Yes. Because if you have a Silverstone Press Pass you can try to catch it at Silverstone on Friday and Saturday (July 19,20) in race trials -- untimed (each day) 10am-11.30am, timed (each day) 1pm-2pm.

Or at the British Grand Prix at Silverstone on July 21. Tricky though: the car does 200 mph plus.

Your easiest bet? **Use the enclosed photograph.**

FREE, with our compliments.

More information:
Peter George
General Services Manager
The Porchester Group
Porchester House
91 Wimpole Street
London W1M 7DA
01-493 9090

More information:
Ken Tyrrell
Tyrrell Racing Organisation Ltd
Long Reach
Ockham
Nr Ripley
Surrey GU23 6PE
04865 4955. Telex. 859146 TYRACE G

Incorporating
PORCHESTER (LONDON) LIMITED, PORCHESTER (BRISTOL) LIMITED, PORCHESTER (MIDLANDS) LIMITED, PORCHESTER (MANCHESTER) LIMITED
PORCHESTER GENERAL INSURANCE SERVICES LIMITED
INSURANCE BROKERS
AND THE PORCHESTER GROUP LIMITED
INCORPORATED IN ENGLAND, REGISTERED NUMBERS 1559346, 1557678, 1556729, 1877843, 1438419 AND 1559780.
Registered offices PORCHESTER HOUSE, 91 WIMPOLE STREET, LONDON W1M 7DA
Directors TREVOR C. DEAVES, TERENCE HARVEY F.L.I.A., MALCOLM MUTKIN F.C.A.

Figure 7.1 Press releases have a high—deservedly high—death rate in newspaper offices. One sure way to lift them out of the usual rut is to illustrate your Press releases.

cast around for other interesting angles, including the use of images.

The opening of a refurbished London restaurant provided another opportunity to use images. The announcement itself and the invitation to a Press party at the restaurant was straightforward enough. I considered the biographies of the owner, his daughter, and the assistant manageress, and the chef/manager sufficiently interesting to rate a separate piece of paper. Their little stories were carefully shaped and justified (squared up on left and right hand margins) by the word processer, to take photo portraits alongside. (See Figure 7.2.)

Gino runs a precision engineering company, selling to ITT, Texas, NEC and other Japanese companies, an achievement that might in itself catch the attention of business editors, if the idea of an industrialist branching out into the restaurant business had not intrigued them sufficiently. Gino's portrait and that of his daughter Sara were headshots. Manager Dino wore a full chef's outfit, including the tall white hat.

When everyone marches to orders

One of the curious discoveries made in the mail-order business is that people march to orders. Tell readers to address their envelope 'Shirt Offer (Dept. DT1)', and that's exactly what they'll do, enabling your staff to file that order as a response to the first ad placed in *The Daily Telegraph*. (If there was a coupon that would carry a similar code, but having it on the envelope may save clerking time.) If you asked people to fill in the coupon only in red ball pen, they would—and you would lose a good number of orders from those who couldn't lay their hands on a red pen!

A similar blind faith attaches to Press releases. One book on Press relations mentions that Press releases are useful because they 'can be kept for a few days', assuming

UPSTAIRS RESTAURANT · PIZZA · PASTA · VINO · **DOWNSTAIRS**

GINO, OWNER, UPSTAIRS/DOWNSTAIRS

When Gino came to London from Rome 24 years ago, it was as an ambitious young man eager to learn the language. Working as a waiter he learned about food and the value, in business, of good service. Meanwhile, the skills that he had worked hard to perfect as an engineering student in Italy, slumbered until 1977 when, with partner George Deacon, he established GG and GD Precision Engineering, specialists in high precision tools for the electronics industry. The boom in demand for such products could not then have been predicted. Today, with bulging order books and a turnover in excess of £1.5 million, Gino takes particular pleasure in telling you how his 50-strong and rapidly expanding South London company sells to Texas Instruments, ITT, NEC and other leading Japanese high tech companies. Now he is fulfilling another dream, that of owning his own restaurant, the cream on this cake being that with Downstairs, the Italian wine bar below the classically English Upstairs restaurant, it is "like owning a little bit of Italy in London".

DINO, MANAGER, UPSTAIRS/DOWNSTAIRS

If there is one culinary tradition that Dino has upheld during his years at Hatchett's, W1 and as Head Chef at the mediaeval Tudor Barn, a noted South London hostelry, it is that hearty eaters deserve to be memorably well fed. Dino promises that Upstairs, specialising in hearty English fare, will be just such a trencherman's delight, offering prime cuts of Scotch beef -- "no other beef will do!" -- bought round the corner at Smithfield, as well as freshly roasted lamb and pork for the off-the-bone carvery. "You won't find microwave ovens, additives or packet sauces here," says Dino, an active member of the Chef & Cooks Circle and the Hotel Catering & Institutional Management Association, "just wholesome, fresh ingredients prepared by people who appreciate good food and enjoy presenting it."

SARA, ASSISTANT MANAGERESS, UPSTAIRS/DOWNSTAIRS

Though barely into her twenties, Sara, daughter of Upstairs/ Downstairs owner Gino, is a committed professional in the catering business. She took her Ordinary National Diploma in Hotel and Catering Management at Westminster College and went on to work first at the London Metropole Hotel, then at the Barkston, latterly a THF establishment. "I liked Barkston's family atmosphere. Staff weren't just names on a payroll, it was small enough to know everybody personally. I believe staff must be motivated and kept in the picture. Our clients were mainly families, too, and that pleased me. We really got close to them and that, to me, is the best way to get customers to come back again and again." That friendly, caring philosophy is something Sara aims to pursue on both sides of the counter at Upstairs/ Downstairs.

Figure 7.2 Using a word processor it is a simple matter to print copy to any given measure and 'justify' (even up) the right-hand side of the text for the sake of neatness. This background information sheet accompanied a more traditional-looking release announcing the opening of a new restaurant close by St Paul's Cathedral.

they are not junked on sight as too boring for a second glance.

But the fact is, if you want the Press to keep something, all you have to do is *ask*. Well, not just ask, but make it *worth their while* to do as you say. When I was announcing some rather mundane internal appointments, promotions within a client company, I could have gone only to the dozen or so industry papers specializing in my client's type of business. But I knew that the company had something big simmering on the back ring, an announcement that would merit a mention in the nationals as well as the trades.

So I sent the client's promotions announcement out to the big boys as well, with this message: 'YOU ARE WELCOME TO RUN THIS NEWS ITEM, RIGHT AWAY. BUT PLEASE FILE IT IN ANY CASE ... MY CLIENT IS ABOUT TO ANNOUNCE A MAJOR NEW VENTURE AND YOU WILL FIND THE BACK-GROUND MATERIAL IN THIS HANDOUT VITAL TO YOU'.

Of course I could have simply enclosed the CV guff with the big story, when it broke. But I'd achieved something much more worthwhile operating this way. I'd *primed* the Press for a humdinger of a story. The nationals don't spend much time with their tongues hanging out for news, but this did prompt several probing phone calls, and when the event did happen, coverage was unusually strong and detailed.

Printing Press releases

Printing Press releases is easy and cheap. I know instant printers who will produce in a couple of hours work in the sort of quantities Press mailings usually go out—not more than a few hundred times a couple of sheets of paper.

Here's how to make your own camera-ready artwork. Take a plain piece of white paper and place it on top of a piece of your own headed stationery. Hold this paper 'sandwich' up to the light. On the plain white paper mark faintly in pencil where your company logo falls, where the registered address runs at the bottom, outline any printed margins or other devices. This shows you how much uncluttered space you have to type in your Press message, insert any image, and so on.

Use a very clear typewriter face for the printing—any of the modern typewriters and many word processors are ideal; the very 'spotty' printing you get in draught mode with a dot-matrix computer printer is *not* acceptable. But a dot matrix that prints letter quality or near letter quality (nlq) will be fine. Your images should be line drawn in dense black ink.

In extremis, if I have to use another colour I choose red: for photographic reasons I won't go into, this reproduces almost as dark as black itself; blue ink sometimes disappears completely. If you want to print a photograph in a Press release you should have it *screened*. The darks, lights and greys of the photograph are turned into tiny dots almost invisible to the naked eye, but under a magnifying glass you'll see that the gradations of light are achieved with varying concentrations of black dots.

The instant print company will normally handle this for you. But it does take time for them to organize, though only half an hour or so to actually do the screening process.

If you are in a searing hurry use the photograph as it is, and if the size isn't right, reduce the image using a photocopier with a reduction facility. The harsh, contrasty image that results reproduces remarkably well. There is now also a stick-on dotted paper, a type of Letraset, that works almost as well as proper screening, and is fine for seat-of-the-pants jobs.

As I say, instant printers are your best bet. But if you really are short of time—or you are on a shoestring budget—go for 'overprinting'. Here, you use a photocopier, substituting the plain white paper for your own headed stationery. Your typed 'artwork' is the image, and this goes against the glass, just as if you were copying any original. The result is your Press release photocopied on to your business stationery. It isn't as crisp as instant printing, but with a good photocopier, it's a good runner-up.

A photocopier is also useful to check artwork you intend sending to a printer. Overprint, as described, to see how the printed version will fit and appear when properly reproduced.

Who should get your Press releases?

Given the amount of wastage involved in mailing a Press release—precious few will win much more than a cursory glance—it makes good business sense to target them as accurately as possible.

For one financial services client I suggested the following breakdown:

- National newspapers, including *The London Standard.*
- Major regional newspapers, such as *The Yorkshire Post.*
- Important weekly papers.
- Insurance trade papers (*Pensions World*, *Money Marketing* etc.).
- Financial trade papers (*Accountancy Age*, etc.).
- Our own 'specials', clients, friendly 'Captains of Industry' and so on.
- Our company's board members and senior personnel.

Publications local to our four UK regional offices; saturation being more important at a local level, this included 'county' magazines. Then there were national and local radio stations, news and features networks, local and national television. The news agencies—Associated Press, Reuters, United Press International.

But who *within* these bodies should receive the release? Send it to the wrong editor or correspondent and you could miss all your chances with a particular medium.

Won't mail get forwarded to the 'right' person, if you get it wrong first time? Often not.

Remember that Press releases as a genre don't rate highly. It may be left to secretaries to decide who should get any second glance. Their news-tasting skills may be less than adequate, especially after the first 50 letters of the day and 10 telephone interruptions.... And the internal communications system of many journalistic offices—yes even top national newspapers—is as sluggish as second class post, or worse.

So it pays you to aim as accurately as you can—and also to use a buckshot technique as a fail safe, especially if you are not sure how the paper might treat your story.

A manufacturer about to launch a television so small it will fit in a signet ring, for example, would need to consider a great number of possibilities. The features editor should be mailed and so should the fashion editor, and the woman's page editor, who often has responsibility for new products. If the TV company was importing hi-tech Japanese parts to fit into British bangles, perhaps the business news editor should also be told. And if the company were raising capital to make or market the product, then the City editor should also be informed. If the new factories would provide new jobs, the industrial editor should know as well.

Even a television reviewer or the entertainments page correspondent might find room for a paragraph and an illustration of this amazing television ring. A photograph, however, might not do justice to so diminutive a product, so the company's Press officers would be better to send their own *line drawing*. And lastly, the best advice is to also mail the editor in person—just in case he or she had a special idea as to how the TV ring should be written up.

DIY Press lists
Of course you can compile your own Press lists, and keep them up to date with a reminder system of postcards. You

write to the correspondents with a note of how you have them classified in your index, ask if the entry is correct, get them to amend if necessary and return the stamped and addressed card to you.

That's how Bill Gibbs of Press release distribution company PNA does it, and I'm sure he won't mind me letting on that the fact that the cards go into a draw with bottles of champagne on offer to the winner has something of a helpful effect in speeding the replies!

How often should you check your list? About every three months for Fleet Street people, though the City has become far more volatile these days, and Pimms, who compete with PNA for business, boast that they were asked to hold off the seating plan for a hospitality luncheon at Wimbledon (business executive's junket) in order to check the job titles of the guests *on the morning of the event!*

There are a number of reference books that will help you scan the market for names of publications and personnel:

- *Benn's Press Dictionary* (Benn Publications Ltd, Directories Division, Union House, Eridge Road, Tunbridge Wells, Kent).
- *Blue Book of British Broadcasting* (Telex Monitors Ltd, 50 Grosvenor Street, London W1X 9FH). Lists programmes, times, staff—or get the information piecemeal from Radio Times and TV Times.
- *BRAD* (British Rate and Data). Mainly for advertising information, but gives a good reference of newspaper and magazine titles, groups of free newspapers, and so on—and it's updated monthly.
- *MediaLink* (PNA, 13/19 Curtain Road, London EC2A 3LT. Tel: 01–377 2521). Invaluable reference work, updated six times a year. Free to valued clients; or £120 a year on subscription, £40 a copy.
- *PRADS Media Lists* (Press Information and Mailing Services Ltd, Greencoat House, Francis Street, London

SW1P 1DH. Tel: 01–828 5502). £65 a month, updated monthly. As with BRAD, subscribers may well discard old copies, as they're encouraged to do by the publishers. You could offer to remove recent back-copies, to save them clogging up their bins, and to save your business some pin money.

How to make sure your release gets to the right person

Ideally, you send a separate Press release, in a separate envelope, to all of your intended targets; to the City editor, industrial editor, shopping editor and so on, if you think all these will find an interesting angle in your story.

But given the wastage of Press mailings, that kind of thoroughness is expensive in terms of stamps, paper, stationery and time. A second best mailing method is to send a batch of releases to the editor's secretary who would do the parcelling out for you.

I sent a release with the message: 'Please pass to appropriate department head, as indicated', and listed below:

The Editor	Features Editor
Arts Galleries Editor	
Financial Editor	Home Shopping Editor

I ringed the relevant names in red felt tip, and was fairly confident that the secretary would march to orders. My release went out in December 1979 and *Homes and Gardens* used it for their issue of July/August for the following year. Clearly there was no chance it would get into the Christmas issue, which had probably been printed or 'gone to bed'—in journalists' parlance—a month before, but nor did we expect our pleasant summer surprise.

Having written your ace Press release what do you do with it?

Get it in the post, fast. Even better, hand deliver it to Fleet Street or wherever your chosen editors have their offices.

Difficult, expensive? Missing deadlines is also a non-cost-effective exercise, that's why I use a mailing company called PNA. They're situated in Curtain Road, EC2, on the edge of the City of London, close to Liverpool Street station, an area which will doubtless be engulfed by financial services people and their communications acolytes in the not-too-distant future.

PNA keep computer records of thousands of editors, city and business editors, features editors, financial writers, and so on, all updated *daily*, along with their changes of title, address and phone numbers. They hand deliver six times a day to Fleet Street, Wapping, etc., and the City, using their own fleet of motorcycle messengers.

To give you an idea how cost-effective using a service like PNA is, their 'Newspac' scheme lets you 'piggy back' (share) a mailing and reach 750 newspaper editors for less than the cost of postage—PNA covers the cost of media selection and addressing, 'stuffing' the envelopes (one of the world's most boring jobs and one for which there is no short cut for small mailings, though you can automate a big run); the envelopes; the postage; and you get a check-list of editors' names and phone numbers, so you can chase the ace, and see what the fate of your release has been.

I suggest you cost out doing such a service in-house. It will be a frightening experience. For the same reason, few people in the rabbit-breeding business also make Davey Crockett hats . . ..

The latest technology puts an end to that time-wasting and frustrating anachronism. The PR communications system par excellence is called *PR Targeter*. I wrote about *PR Targeter* for the company marketing it, PNA:

REMARKABLE NEW SYSTEM HELPS BUSY PRs DO MORE AND BETTER BUSINESS

Suppose the whole business of writing, targeting and distributing Press releases could be made simpler, quicker, more cost effective ... and the means of achieving these time and money-saving benefits were available to you now. Wouldn't it make sense to find out more about such an advantageous system?

Indeed it would. Especially as such a system has in fact been developed and is available to you immediately and at remarkably low cost.

PR Targeter, as the system is known, is a computer-based 'tool' of the trade designed specifically for the professional PR executive.

PR Targeter is a complete desk-top media and communications system, incorporating telex, electronic mail, media databank, automatic telephone management, and more. It is based on a desk-top computer ... and a unique software program, which carries virtually all of the information contained in PNA's comprehensive databank of UK Press, radio and TV contacts. You are already familiar with this information in its printed version as PR Planner and PNA MediaLink.

PR Targeter puts all of this information at your fingertips, on screen, at the touch of a button. Scanning the media lists, selecting your mailing options—including your own private and 'bespoke' lists, which can also be programmed in—is a swift and painless activity. As easy, in fact, as paging the Oracle!

Then key in your Press release and word process it to perfection. If you want to study previous releases, you can summon them from *PR Targeter's* prodigious memory. You can print 'hard' copy to rework on the train, take home, or post to someone.

Because *PR Targeter* is linked to a nationwide electronic mailing system, you can quickly transmit your copy and choice of media selections direct to PNA ... to your client .... You can even send a copy of your release electronically to Press clippings agency Romeike & Curtice. Or you can opt to print out your own gummed labels.

Whatever course you choose, you must save time. And if you decide to use PNA's printing and distribution services (which include hourly deliveries to the major media and the City), you can achieve your objectives without leaving the desk or talking on the phone.

In fact the only demands on you are your brain-power and a little finger-walking over some keys.

How to write Press releases that really hit the spot*

'I try to throw away Press releases unread', quipped Londoner's Diary in *the London Evening Standard*. The fact is, they all get read—or at least scanned—though few see light of print. We rang around the national papers for some positive advice from news editors.

Daily Express, News Editor Philippa Kennedy: 'There must be a clear-cut headline, so we can see instantly what it's about followed by clear, punchy paragraphs. Releases are really just tasters. Write just enough to make us want to know more, after all, we get about 100 per day.'

Key points? 'A date and time on top, *underlined* ... whether there's a picture facility ... are people available for interviews .... The first page can be short, with more detailed information on a second sheet ... a name, address and contact phone number is a must .... Embargoes are sensible on some occasions, but they can make a story seem more important than it is.'

The Independent, City Editor David Brewerton: 'I dislike Press releases where the writer is trying to tell me the story without sticking to the facts. Releases written as news stories—in what someone thinks is a newsy style—are worse than useless, they're so difficult to re-write. The merchant banks and some public relations organizations are very good. They give the details of a takeover, for example, and then a bit of background to the deal. That's what I prefer.'

*Taken from *PNA Newsletter*, November/December 1986.

'We welcome pictures and use them if our backs are against the wall, though we prefer to take our own. One thing that does irritate: if you try to contact someone and they're not at the end of the phone. If they're on paper as a contact, they should be there. We live with embargoes, but I prefer not to have them at all.'

London Daily News, City Editor Jim Levi: 'It should be clear what it's all about at first glance. Clever headings are irritating. Pictures are useful, a phone number, *and* an out-of-hours number are vital. Embargoes should be avoided where possible, though I appreciate that people want to manage their news to some degree.'

The Guardian, Assistant News Editor Paul Johnson: 'Length isn't important, we can digest long pieces and judge the interest. We'll rearrange the news points anyway. What does annoy is having to plough through material that isn't worthwhile: there's a certain lack of discrimination when releases are sent out.'

Today News Desk (the paper has a 'no names, no pack drill' policy): 'Our main complaint: people send in releases that haven't a snowball's chance in hell of getting into the paper. Two or three people go through all of them every morning. They're read and assessed, but about 80 per cent go in the bin. The worst offenders are new product announcements that are sheer advertising. Why don't they buy space?'

How to home in on provincial press targets*

How's your success rate in the provinces? Do you find that London titles are easier targets for your Press releases—against all the odds?

'It could be that you don't know enough about the pride and prejudices of out-of-town editors', says Don Wood, former Syndication Editor of United Newspapers.

Syndication is the business of retailing specific features

*Taken from *PNA Newsletter*, March/April 1987.

again and again. So, for example, a piece that appears in the *London Standard* is still an unknown quantity to readers of the *Yorkshire Evening Post*, and can be sold and published there to equal effect.

Don spent fifteen years as Syndication Editor of United Newspapers, running their features syndication office in Fleet Street, and supplying the *Yorkshire Post . . . Sheffield Star . . . Liverpool Post . . .* and many, many more well-respected regional journals. (He is now working on the Short Course for the National Council for the Training of Journalists, Carlton House, Hemnall Street, Epping, Essex.)

'News releases can be sent out *ad hoc*', says Don. But a Press release with a features flavour—especially those designed to be used 'as is'—needs careful thought and a more bespoke treatment.

Syndication feature
Here are his tips:

1. Clearly it helps to establish a good relationship with an editor (or correspondent). But how many PR people follow through, when they have had a write-up, with a letter or phone call? Find out what editors like and need—and send them more of it.
2. Don't 'double up'. You might consider it a great coup, to get your client into both the *Wolverhampton Express & Star* and the *Birmingham Evening Mail* on the same day. However, their circulation areas overlap in part, and the editors won't thank you for making them wear the same hats. The answer . . .?
3. Either send out radically differently written stories, albeit on the same topic. Or leave out one conflicting party in your initial mailing. Check for response, over the phone; if negative, then mail the rival paper. That way you upset nobody.
4. The provincial Press is very parochial. They're proud

of it and they are getting more parochial. Out-of-area features content is minimal, usually. Your best chance of getting in is to include a local angle. How . . .?

5. Cultivate a local correspondent/photographer. If your client is running a marathon competition, for example, get your 'stringer' to find some local worthies prepared to take up the challenge.

6. If your story relates to a retail product, be sure local shops have the goods in stock—and say so in your copy.

7. Study the papers you're mailing to. That is the only way to learn about preferred style and length (rarely over 800 words) of features copy. If the editorial department won't oblige by sending back numbers, ask the advertisement manager for a few, together with a rate card. You'll find he's rather more highly motivated!

8. Always try to include a photograph or drawing. Illustrated Press releases have a much higher success rate, wherever a paper circulates.

9. Free papers are 'softer' targets. That doesn't mean they'll include a puff in the second para. But they are cost-conscious, and your usable copy saves them time and money.

10. Include a reply-paid postcard. Ask: Did you like the piece? Will you use it? When? Would you like to receive more?

11. Where appropriate, consider staging regional Press launches, injecting a local flavour, when you can. Most local papers don't have the staff or funds to cover London launches, but they will thank you for bringing your stories to them.

Conflict of interest
These are the major clashes. *Manchester Evening News/ Bolton Evening News; Manchester Evening News/Liverpool Echo; Yorkshire Post/Northern Echo.*

The biggest circulating evening papers include: the *Wolverhampton Express & Star*, *Birmingham Evening Mail*, *Manchester Evening News*, *Liverpool Echo*, *Leicester Mercury*, *Yorkshire Evening Post*, *Sheffield Star*, *Bristol Evening Post*. Certain morning papers—such as the *Western Daily Press*, *Western Morning News* and *Liverpool Post*—see themselves as combined local/national papers.

The three main Scottish papers are the *Daily Record*, *The Scotsman* and the *Glasgow Herald*. The second is Edinburgh-orientated, the latter more southerly in scope. But each considers itself to be a 'national' paper for Scotland. So you should never double up by sending the same copy to each paper at the same time: you could lose two potential good friends.

If you get a hammering in the Press
If you ever get a bad write-up in the papers, don't lose your rag. It happens. Remember the old adage: all publicity is good publicity. This may not immediately hold true. But given time, the public tends to remember the name of the maligned company and forget the mud.

What should you do?
Stay calm: take quick, deep breaths in, slow breaths out—an old Karate trick. Above all, *don't reach for the phone to call the editor.*

The sensible thing to do—often overlooked in the heat of the moment—is to do what you would normally do in *any* crisis, such as a financial shenanigan, fire at the works, accident and so on.

Call a meeting of the board or whoever else you turn to for expert help and advice in the good times. At once. Talk through the crisis ... assess the damage. Consult a solicitor, if need be. Then act—fast.

The normal course is for the managing director to write a letter. Unless the MD is a whizz at writing, and normally handles the firm's writing load, this is a mistake. The person to write a letter to the editor is the person you respect and regularly pay to write your copy. What is needed here is the professional touch, a measured response from someone who is trained to be detached from a situation.

MDs and other bosses may be spot on in their business instincts, in calmer moments. When it comes to the crunch they often make the following mistakes when launching into print.

They ... think too much. 'The more you tell, the more you sell', is true of advertising copy. With letters to the editor, 'The more you think, the more you sink', is the rule. The more you protest your innocence the more guilty you become—in the eyes of the Press.

Find where the story is flawed with errors of fact, and hammer away at that. Journalists pride themselves on their accuracy, and you will touch a raw nerve.

Thinking also slows you down. The aim is to act quickly. If necessary, send a holding letter, to give you time to investigate the allegations more fully.

Keep copy short. Business letters, other than sales letters, ought to be crisp. The same when writing to the Press. If you are writing for publication say so. If your letter is not for publication say that, too.

If a member of your staff is involved, and is at fault, say that the person concerned has been disciplined or sacked. Every barrel has its rotten apple; don't try to turn yours into cider.

If faulty goods are the problem, make a full reparation to the customer who reported on you. Find out what they want—fresh goods, full cash refund, or whatever—and, if possible, give it to them. Without delay.

Then trumpet your actions to the editor—in a letter or Press release. Perhaps even with a photograph of the customer receiving the gift.

It's curious, but true: editors don't always know where their bread is buttered. They build their reputation on having their finger on the pulse of the populace, and then run amok when one reader writes a nasty letter.

I was feeding a provincial paper with stories which were proving to be popular with the readers and good news for my client, too. One article drew over 100 phone calls to the client—and the phone number had not even been mentioned in the article. No doubt, some readers turned to the paper for help in tracing the company. However, when one reader took offence at an angle in the copy, the whole project was called into question!

If it makes sense, open your doors to the Press. Challenge them to come to your premises and investigate their ill-founded claims. If the paper that is 'agin' you refuses your invitation you can sometimes play them off against a rival newspaper in the same circulation area.

Journalists don't normally like to get closely involved with the advertising department—not even if the ads pay their salaries. But it's a fact of life that you are less likely to get a pasting in the papers which regularly take your ads. So turn to the paper that knows and loves you for redress. And when the heat dies down, see that *all* parties get a share of the advertising cake.

Should you threaten legal action? Calling in the law is a bit like writing a long letter: the assumption will be made that you are guilty as charged. On the other hand, many local papers are run on a shoestring, go into a flap at the prospect of an expensive court case, and will call off the dogs.

But if you lose money as a result of bad publicity, once you call in the solicitors, one thing is sure: you will start to lose even more—in legal bills.

8. *How to motivate yourself to write*

Curiously I find writing is the least time-consuming activity in my business. In fact, I spend very little time in the 'bum on chair, fingers on keyboard' writing position. Much more of my day is spent on the phone ... chasing people ... writing letters ... hounding debtors ... and so on. But the product I have to sell, my writing (often in association with consulting skills) can only be made—literally *hand-made*—on the desk, at the typewriter/word processor.

It's so easy to convince myself that because I have been running around all day, and possibly have even won worthwhile commissions, and feel tired to boot, that I have actually done some work. Essential as such activity is, though, it doesn't pay any bills. Only the yards of paper that stream out of the back of my writing machine does that.

Not surprisingly, I, and other professional writers like me, have devised a number of techniques for getting, and keeping, these writing juices flowing. They may work for you, too.

'Most deals don't make'

Most deals don't make. You must have heard that expression—or something similar to it. It's simply a statement of fact about business life. You work away at any number of business deals and, on balance, clinch very few of them.

The fault may not be your own. You put your best foot

forward, pitch your best shots, but still you cannot pull off the business. The reason may be the other party pulls out, or circumstances beyond your control, such as the weather (you are in the umbrella business and you run into a dry spring) screw you up; the state of the economy (you deal in collectable 'busted bonds', share certificates that have been dishonoured by the ruling Russian regime these past 60-odd years, and suddenly the Party decides to pay compensation!)—*anything* can kill a deal stone dead. And experience reveals that, by and large, deals follow Murphy's law, which states that if something can go wrong, it will go wrong.

That jam-buttered toast that falls from the breakfast table will end up jam-side down. You know it, and I know it. So what do we do about it?

Well, two things. Firstly, we spend our time and energy concentrating on those activities which, based on experience, look as if they *might* pay off. And secondly, we are prolific. We try to do a *lot* of deals. If the eye is on the target ... the will is strong ... and there's enough money in the kitty ... the active business executive profits from aggressive energy. This can be selling in the field ... advertising ... hitting prospects with direct mail shots ... what have you. The same is true of writing.

Here are some of the ways in which, I, and other professional writers, get down to work and ensure that we keep at it, regardless of writer's cramp, block or what have you. Not all of these methods will suit you. It depends on temperament ... mood ... practice ... and so on. But at least try them and see what happens.

1. When is the best time of the day to work at writing? The same time as is best for just about any kind of activity: first thing in the morning. Why? 'Because if you do it, it's done.' This isn't metaphysics, but an insight into human nature. As time goes by, a million other things will clamour for your attention.

Besides which, as the day wears on, so do you. Accomplishing *anything* becomes more of a chore.

2. Another early bird perk: when you start early, there are fewer people around to interrupt ... the phones won't have started, and more. ... You'll feel smart, for having stolen a march on the rest of the slumbering world.

3. 'Start early' and 'start now' should be taken to their logical conclusion. Let *nothing* slip between you and your writing paper or terminal screen.

4. One of my more intriguing privileges has been to teach journalism to young students at the London College of Fashion. They were hungry for knowledge, and through my lessons had come to appreciate the value of being prolific.

   'How do you get things done ... how do you manage to write, day in, day out', one 20-year-old asked. I told her I got up early and simply got stuck in.

   'What, straight after breakfast?' she said.

   'No', I explained, 'straight out of bed, unwashed, unkempt and unfed.'

   That part is essential: *nothing* must come between you and your objective.

   I told her I had learned the trick from the famous classical guitarist Julian Bream, whom I'd interviewed for the 'Life in the Day of' page in *The Sunday Times* colour magazine. Whenever Bream was coming up to a concert, he knew he had to exercise his fingers, using a gruelling series of scales.

   It was a drudge, it took an hour and a half. But there was no short cut. So he did it as he got up—mind you, Bream did say he washed his hands first, and also took a cup of tea into his chapel-studio!

   Having got that finger-flexing chore out of the way, he would reward himself with a real old English fry-up of a breakfast—and to hell with the calories!

5. Start early ... and beat Parkinson's Law. C. Northcote

Parkinson, an economics don, studied people at work. He came to the conclusion—amazing, but true—that work 'expands' to fill the time available to do it in. This explains why the typist with just one letter to write before lunch just manages to slip it into the boss before the Great Escape.

And why that same typist, with six letters to type before lunch, just manages to get the sixth missive Tippexed to perfection as the eating exodus begins!

How does starting early trounce PL? Only in that everything else you have to do in your day, other than your writing, is, *of itself*, quite capable of filling up all the time available to you. Write first, and there should still be time to do everything else. You'll need to move a bit faster, that's all.

6. I said 'early'—first thing—is the best time to get started. The more disciplined may be able to tune into their biorhythms and still come out on top.

One of the surprising things we discover about time is that there are different sorts. Some of it is good time: you're in tip-top form, able to steam through tasks. Other times are a washout—even watching TV seems like hard work!

Keep a diary and note how you feel at different times of the day. Over a week or two you'll see a pattern come clear. You may be at your peak in the morning—or you may be a bright, night owl. By knowing your energy swings and moods you can pick the best time to help you achieve more.

When you're button bright, that's the time to put by for important, high concentration activities like writing. Second-rate time, such as after lunch on a Sunday, may be suitable for revising your writing. But if you ever feel 'good for nothing', then maybe that's the best thing to do.

7. Get started! Once you do, the creative juices will flow. There is something inexorable about work under way.

You'll do a bit more, and a bit more. Soon you will bite the head off anyone who interrupts your progress.

8. If you must put your work to one side, end in the middle of a sentence. When you return to your desk you will be able to finish that sentence without a moment's anxiety or hesitation. And the next sentence will flow from your fingertips.

9. If you can't make any headway with the job in hand, write something else. The mere act of writing can help the flow. In extremis, type any old sentence, type any old sentence . . . .

10. Do the easy parts first. It will give you courage and confidence to move on to the 'nightmare zone'.

11. All the books say structure your piece of writing . . . write a resumé of the sales letter you intend to write, and so on.

    In reality, writing a synopsis, or making a list of what needs to be done, may be a way of *avoiding* getting started. So start *anywhere*.

12. Small, in writing, is beautiful. You may not know the beginning or the end of your writing project. But you must know *something* you want to say. So write that down.

    War And Peace may be one of the greatest novels ever written. But it really is no more than a string of sentences assembled in a particular way. If you can write one sentence or heading, you are on your way.

13. Pre-empt the temptation to skive. . . . As a student, my ex-wife would surround herself with everything she could possibly need to reward or sustain herself while she worked: cigarettes, flask of coffee, sandwiches, chocolate, and so on. That way, there was rarely any excuse to stir from the desk.

    She studied her way to a PhD in psychology, so she was clearly getting something right.

14. 'When should a writer have the first drink of the day?' is a question I like to put to my writing students.

'Before breakfast,' one quipped. 'Right!' I said, 'If that's what works, do it.'

If you are single-minded enough to start writing with the milkman, you will probably be tough enough to overcome your alcoholism.

15. Tell someone you respect, and who is *au fait* with the job in hand, that you are going to do it. Preferably state that you will accomplish your written work by a specific time or date.

    It's easy to make excuses to yourself. We let ourselves get away with this sort of cheating because it's private. We know we've broken faith, but no one else does, so it matters less. That's why it pays to involve others when committing yourself to a major writing task.

    If you need an example of the effectiveness of this 'confessional' method, look at the phenomenal success of that self-help slimming organization known as 'Weight Watchers'.

16. It's easier to order bits of paper than your thoughts. Once you've committed all the jigsaw pieces of your writing—the headlines, sentences, chapters—to paper, juggling these to make a coherent structure can be pure pleasure.

    Stitching the thoughts together so the joins don't show is as nothing once the material is *there*.

Slogans which help spur you on

A surprising number of successful people find self-motivating slogans a powerful driving force. Not a Bible-load of them, just a few well chosen ones. Moe Jenns, who was managing director of an advertising agency while still in her early thirties, had this legend, framed, on her desk. 'Don't go to bed angry: stay up and fight.'

Then there are the quips that are almost a part of business folklore—though they still hit the target, years on, such as: 'When the going gets tough; the tough get going.'

Trevor Deaves, the 34-year-old managing director of The Porchester Group, the UK's biggest independent life brokerage, is a great fan of slogans—and one of the most motivated men I ever met. He takes the 'Tough' adage and turns it on its head. 'When the going gets tough,' quips Mr Deaves, 'Something's going wrong!'

Tax and investment consultant R. J. Temple used this to head up a recent mailing to get people to put cash into their unit trust scheme: 'Money doesn't always bring happiness. People with $10 million are no happier than people with $9 million!'

Try these for size:

- 'Do it now!'
- 'Don't get angry. Get even.'
- 'There are no business failures—Only people failures.'
- 'When a man doesn't know what harbour he is making for, no wind is the right wind.'
- 'How you think today determines what you will be, and where you will be tomorrow.'
- 'You only get tired when you're losing.'
- 'Success is a journey, not a destination.'

Slogans that point up the fleeting nature of time are especially potent. 'Don't be one of those people who has more time than money', says it nicely. 'Winners are just competitors who never quit' is a reminder of the need for perseverence, the most important single trait for success, according to Heron boss Gerald Ronson.

To close, how does this grab you: Will you be one of those people whose epitaph reads, 'Could have tried harder?'

9. Seven reasons why designers get my coat, but not my vote

Don't get me wrong. I love good design, and go out of my way to find and buy it; I spend hundreds of pounds on Italian 'uplighting'; I wear a Swedish-styled Barbour, shave with a matt black German razor; and all the rest of it. But when it comes to my copy, I'd rather *I* was in charge than the designer.

Look at it this way—I drive an Italian car, but would I want an Italian chauffeur?

In truth, some of my best friends are designers and art directors. Nevertheless, from time to time I have to remind them that there is scant evidence of a designer ever having sold anything from the printed page. That job always seems to be the work of the wordsmith.

That said, we must accept that the designer's star is in the ascendant, and if we can't fight them, let's at least try to outflank them. These are some of the areas which can become a battleground.

- The designers are 'creative' people. They crave to be different. Everything we know about people and what moves them to respond, to buy from us, vote for us, confirms that people are the same the world over and are largely motivated by the *same* fundamental desires.
- One of the ways designers like to be different is to 're-verse out' type. This means printing the words in white on a dark background, rather than the normal dark

lettering on a light background (as this book, your morning paper, etc.).

'Research shows that people find reading reversed-out copy hard work: they're simply not used to it. There is one exception where reversed-out type is acceptable, however. For short headlines.

- Another favourite designer trick is to print copy on top of an illustration (see Figure 9.1). If you want people to read your words without having to turn on foglights, don't let this happen.
- A picture is worth a thousand words, it is said. So why waste any words on a picture? This must be why designers like pictures without captions. How would you feel about watching a TV documentary with no commentary at all?
- Designers sometimes like to be witty. That's why they print the title to a picture of ⅄ƎN⅟ꓷIS upside down (an actual example). What would your response be if you went into a shop and the sales assistant greeted you standing on his head? (Mind you, that would at least be *original*.)
- Designers like short copy, big print. Or short copy, big pictures. Research assures us that long copy sells more.
- Tests prove that mail order ads that feature a coupon pull a better response, resulting in more orders, more enquiries, more leads, and so on. Therefore, it must make sense to use good-size coupons that are easy to fill in. Some designers find coupons old fashioned, a blot on their masterpiece. So they leave them off; make them too small to write in; or turn them into triangles across the bottom corner of the page.

Of course, all this is sure to upset a few people, and besides, it is only my opinion. *Wrong!* I have an ally in advertising legend David Ogilvy, whose agency, Ogilvy & Mather, is one of the largest in the world. In *Ogilvy on Advertising* he writes:

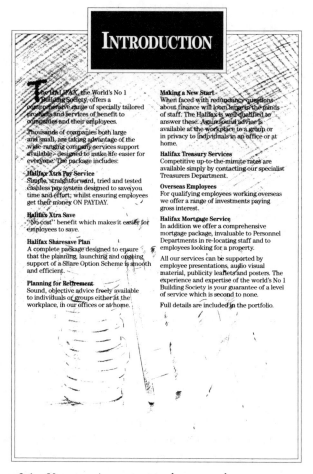

Figure 9.1 You owe it to your readers to make your copy easy to read. And if you are promoting your own products you owe even more to yourself to make sure your audience reads your words. In the inserts included in their 'Company Services Portfolio' package the Halifax Building Society (the world's biggest) appears to have abandoned themselves to the mercies of a somewhat self-indulgent designer. 'Overprinting'—printing on a colour base or a picture or design—is always a hazardous activity. Black on white is the formula that works. The closer you stick to that the better your printed material will work for you. The drive to be different and 'creative' is another dangerous urge. This too should be controlled.

There is no law which says that advertisements have to look like advertisements. If you make them look like editorial pages, you will attract more readers. Roughly six times as many people read the average article as the average advertisement.

Very few advertisements are read by more than one reader in twenty. I conclude that editors communicate better than admen.

Look at the news magazines which have been successful in attracting readers: *Time* and *Newsweek* in the United States, *L'Express* and *Le Point* in France, *Der Spiegel* in Germany, *L'Espresso* in Italy, *Cambio 16* in Spain. They all use the same graphics:

- Copy has priority over illustrations.
- The copy is set in a serif type like this book [and like *this* book].
- Every photograph has a caption.
- The copy starts with drop-initials.
- The type is set black on white.

Now look at the advertisements in the same magazines. You will see that:

- Illustrations are given priority over copy.
- The copy is often set in sans serif, which is hard to read: we are accustomed to serifs in books, magazines and newspapers.
- The copy is often set in one column of 120 characters or more—too wide to be readable.
- Few of the photographs have captions, because the art directors are not aware that four times as many people read captions as body copy.
- There are very few drop-initials, because the art directors are not aware that they increase readership.
- The copy is frequently set in reverse—white on black. I have even seen *coupons* set in reverse; you

cannot fill them out unless you have white ink in the house.

One painful, early experience taught me a lot of things. About designers, working with print and publicity, and also about people. I was writing a series of advertising and promotional pieces for a company in the business of selling rabbits for meat. The company sold breeding rabbits and farming know-how, and the rabbits just got on with producing the meat—off their own backs—as rabbits do.

I wrote a letter, a few trade paper ads, and I also wrote a brochure. The brochure was a masterpiece of research and application. When I finished my story—all about how the French army, in particular, were crying out for rabbit meat; how rabbits could be fed on pellets, not messy expensive greens; how you could build 'tower-block' homes for breeding rabbits, so little floor area was needed—I had become a world authority on the subject. More to the point, I was sure I had written a thoroughly convincing sales story which would pull in orders.

I teamed up with a designer, known to me for years, a personal friend, in fact. Up to that point he had been the best sort of designer: he worked with flair and in a sympathetic way, but he also knew how to 'march to orders'.

The brochure went through all the print stages, I passed the proofs. No mention was ever made of colour and I assumed it would be black and white. When the brochure finally appeared, it was green. Not only was the cover green, but all the print inside was green, so leafy green in fact that you could barely read it, and most people, I suspected, would not even want to try.

I asked my designer friend why he had done this. 'Well,' he giggled, 'green . . . for rabbits, rabbits, greens . . .'. From that moment on, I took no chances with designers. I suggest you do the same and:

1. Spell out how you want things to be.

2. If you don't understand something, ask questions and keep asking them until you get satisfactory answers.
3. Monitor *every* stage of the print process. The one you let slide will be the one that goes wrong.

Recommended reading

The majority of the books listed below are out of print. Some are quite old. No matter. Writers, especially American writers, have known all about winning writing techniques for about a century, as far as I can work out; and have been expressing it in familiar ways for at least 50 years. But that still leaves the problem of getting hold of them.

There are a number of ways of finding out-of-print books—major public libraries are extremely helpful. In London the Camden Library, Rosebery Avenue, WC1, are tireless in their pursuit of written exotica. You may find similar paragons in your area.

The method is to fill in a form with as much details of publication as possible. You pay a small 'finding fee'. It can take a few weeks or months if the book is American. It's worth the wait.

Alternatively—and much better to my mind, as I scrawl all over my books—you can use book-tracing specialists.

- Hatchards, 187 Piccadilly, London W1.
- W & A Houben, 2 Church Court, Richmond, Surrey.
- Leon Drucker, 25 Dicey Avenue, London NW2.
- Bibliagora, PO Box 7, Hounslow, Middlesex, TW3 2LA.
- Hammersmith Books, Barnes High Street, London SW13.
- Out of Print, 17 Fairwater Grove, East Cardiff, Wales.

For more information on stockists of American books write to the US Information Service, Reference and Research Library, 55/56 Upper Brook Street, London W1A 2LH.

To advertise for specific books use the pages of *Clique*, the trade paper for book dealers. Write to Clique Limited, 75 World's End Road, Handsworth Wood, Birmingham, B20 2NS.

Selected recommended reading

Bermont, Hubert, *How To Become A Successful Consultant In Your Own Field*, Bermont Books, 1978.

Bermont, Hubert, *The Successful Consultant's Guide To Authoring, Publishing and Lecturing*, Bermont Books, 1979.

Bermont, Hubert, *The Successful Consultant's Guide To Writing Proposals and Reports*, Bermont Books, 1979.

Berry, Thomas Elliott, *The Craft of Writing*, McGraw-Hill, 1974.

Blanchard, Kenneth, Johnson, Spencer, *The One Minute Manager*, Fontana/Collins, 1982.

Breen, George, Blankenship, A. B. *Marketing Research*, McGraw-Hill Book Company, 1982.

Butterfield, William H., *The Business Letter In Modern Form*, Prentice-Hall, 1938.

Campbell, Charles, *The Writers' Reference Book*, TV Boardman and Company, 1963.

Cannon, Tom, *How To Win Profitable Business*, Business Books, 1984.

Cassels, J. W. W., *Direct Mail*, Business Publications, 1950.

Coulson-Thomas, Colin, *Public Relations Is Your Business*, The Anchor Press Limited, 1981.

Farrar, Larston, *How to Make $18,000 A Year Free-Lance Writing*, Hawthorn Books, 1957.

Flesch, Rudolf, *The Way To Write*, McGraw-Hill Book Company, 1947.

Funk, Wilfred, *Six Weeks To Words Of Power*, Pocket Books, 1953.

Geffner, Andrea B., *Business English*, Barron's Educational Series, 1982.

Greb, Walter, *How To Build Your Own Mail Order Business*, 1950.

Gunning, Robert, *The Technique Of Clear Writing*, McGraw-Hill Book Company, 1952.

Gunther, Max, *Writing The Modern Magazine Article*, The Writer, 1968.

Harral, Stewart, *The Features Writer's Handbook*, University Of Oklahoma Press, 1958.

Hill, Napoleon, *How To Sell Your Way Through Life*, Psychology Publishing Co Ltd, 1946.

How To Sell By Mail, General Publications, 1943.

How To Write Letters That Win, A. W. Shaw Company, 1912.

Hukson, Howard Penn, *Publishing Newsletters*, Charles Scribner's Sons, 1982.

Hull, Raymond, *How To Write 'How-To' Books and Articles*, Poplar Press, 1981.

Lakein, Alan, *How To Get Control Of Your Life*, David McKay Company, 1974.

Laird, Donald A., and Laird, Elenor C., *The Techniques of Delegating*, McGraw-Hill Book Company, 1957.

Lewis, Mel, *How To Make Money From Antiques*, Blandford Press, 1981.

Lewis, Mel, *How To Collect Money That Is Owed To You*, McGraw-Hill Book Company, 1982.

Maas, Jane, *Better Brochures, Catalogs And Mailing Pieces*, St Martins's press, 1981.

McCrimmon, James M., *Writing With A Purpose*, Houghton Mifflin Company, 1950.

Mort, Simon, *How To Write A Successful Report*, Business Books, 1983.

Neal, James M., and Brown, Suzanne S., *Newswriting And Reporting*, The Iowa State University Press, 1976.

Ogilvy, David, *Confessions Of An Advertising Man*, Longmans Green And Co, 1963.

Ogilvy, David, *Ogilvy On Advertising*, Pan Books, 1983.

Parkinson, C. Northcote and Rowe, Nigel, *Communicate*, Prentice Hall, 1977.

Provost, Gary, *Make Every Word Count*, Writers Digest Books, 1964.

Ringer, Robert J., *Winning Through Intimidation*, Futura Publications, 1973.

Ruff, Howard J., *How To Prosper During The Coming Bad Years*, Times Books, 1979.

Shurter, Robert L., *Effective Letters In Business*, McGraw-Hill Book Company, 1948.

Simon, Julian L., *How To Start and Operate a Mail-Order Business*, McGraw-Hill Book Company, 1965.

Successful Local Avertising, Chartsearch Limited, 1981.

Webster, Kuswa, *Sell Copy*, Writers Digest Books, 1979.

Wells, Gordon, *How To Communicate*, McGraw-Hill Book Company, 1978.

Wheeler, Elmer, *Tested Sentences That Sell*, The World's Work, 1953.

White, Roderick, *Advertising What It Is And How To Do It*, McGraw-Hill Book Company, 1980.

Winston, Stephanie, *The Organized Executive*, W. W. Norton & Company, 1983.

Wolf, Janet L., *What Makes Women Buy*, McGraw-Hill Book Company, 1958.

Index